Pearson Revise

T0345769

Pearson Edexcel GCSE (9–1)

Biology

Foundation tier

Revision Guide

Series Consultant: Harry Smith

Authors: Pauline Lowrie and Sue Kearsey

A note from the publisher

In order to ensure that this resource offers high-quality support for the associated Pearson qualification, it has been through a review process by the awarding body. This process confirms that this resource fully covers the teaching and learning content of the specification or part of a specification at which it is aimed. It also confirms that it demonstrates an appropriate balance between the development of subject skills, knowledge and understanding, in addition to preparation for assessment.

Endorsement does not cover any guidance on assessment activities or processes (e.g. practice questions or advice on how to answer assessment questions), included in the resource nor does it prescribe any particular approach to the teaching or delivery of a related course.

While the publishers have made every attempt to ensure that advice on the qualification and its assessment

is accurate, the official specification and associated assessment guidance materials are the only authoritative source of information and should always be referred to for definitive guidance.

Pearson examiners have not contributed to any sections in this resource relevant to examination papers for which they have responsibility.

Examiners will not use endorsed resources as a source of material for any assessment set by Pearson.

Endorsement of a resource does not mean that the resource is required to achieve this Pearson qualification, nor does it mean that it is the only suitable material available to support the qualification, and any resource lists produced by the awarding body shall include this and other appropriate resources.

For the full range of Pearson revision titles across KS2, 11+, KS3, GCSE, Functional Skills, AS/A Level and BTEC visit:
www.pearsonschools.co.uk/revise

A small bit of small print

Pearson Edexcel publishes Sample Assessment Material and the Specification on its website. This is the official content and this book should be used in conjunction with it. The worked examples and questions in this book have been written to help you practise the topics in the specification, and to help you prepare for your exams. Remember that the real exam questions may not look like this, and the questions in this book will not appear in your exams.

Contents

A small bit of small print

Edexcel publishes Sample Assessment Material and the Specification on its website. This is the official content and this book should be used in conjunction with it. The questions in Now try this have been written to help you practise every topic in the book. Remember: the real exam questions may not look like this.

Plant and animal cells

Animals and plants are formed from **cells**. Animal cells and plant cells have some parts in common. These parts have particular functions in a cell. Cells like these, with a nucleus and membrane-bound organelles such as mitochondria, are called eukaryotic cells.

Generalised structures

Generalised animal cell

Generalised plant cell

Cell membrane: controls what enters and leaves the cell, e.g. oxygen, carbon dioxide, glucose

Nucleus: a large structure that contains genes that control the activities of the cell

Cytoplasm: jelly-like substance that fills the cell – many reactions take place here

Mitochondria (single: mitochondrion): tiny structures where respiration takes place, releasing energy for cell processes

Ribosomes (present in the cytoplasm but not visible at this size): where proteins are made (protein synthesis)

cell wall

central vacuole

chloroplasts

Worked example

Name the three structures that are found in most plant cells but not animal cells, and describe their functions. **(4 marks)**

Chloroplasts are the structures where photosynthesis takes place to make food for the plant cell.

The cell wall is made of cellulose, and is tough so that it helps support the cell and helps it keep its shape.

The large central vacuole contains cell sap, which helps to keep the plant cell rigid.

> 1 mark is for naming the three structures and there is 1 mark for each function.

> Watch out! The cell membrane and cell wall are different and separate structures.

Now try this

1 Muscle cells contain more mitochondria than skin cells. Suggest why. **(3 marks)**

2 State the names of four structures found in both plant cells and animal cells. **(4 marks)**

3 Suggest an explanation for why not all plant cells have chloroplasts. **(2 marks)**

Different kinds of cell

Some plant and animal cells are **specialised** for different functions. Bacteria have a different kind of **cell structure** from plant and animal cells.

Bacterial cells

Bacteria have a simple cell structure. Like animal and plant cells, they have a cell membrane surrounding the cytoplasm. But they do not have a nucleus. These are called prokaryotic cells.

A single loop of **chromosomal DNA** lies free in the cytoplasm. This carries most of the bacterial genes.

cell membrane

Some bacteria have a **flagellum** to help them move.

Ribosomes are tiny structures that make proteins.

Some bacteria have extra circles of DNA called **plasmid DNA**. Plasmids contain additional genes that are not found in chromosomes.

Many bacteria have a **cell wall** for protection, but it is made of different substances to plant cell walls.

Worked example

(a) Egg cells and sperm cells contain haploid nuclei. Explain how this is related to the function of these cells. **(2 marks)**

A haploid nucleus contains half the genetic information needed by an organism. When a sperm cell fuses with an egg cell, a diploid zygote is formed with all the genetic information needed for an organism.

(b) For each of the three cells shown, explain one specialisation related to its function. Do not include ideas about the nucleus. **(3 marks)**

The egg cell contains nutrients in the cytoplasm to supply the growing embryo. The sperm cell has a tail for swimming to the egg cell for fertilisation. Epithelial cells line tubes, such as the trachea. Cilia move things along the tube, such as mucus. This cell has a lot of cilia to move mucus, containing dirt and bacteria, away from the lungs.

Make sure that you can recognise an unusual feature of a cell, which may be a specialisation to allow the cell to carry out a particular function. For example, in a sperm cell the acrosome contains enzymes to digest a way through the egg cell membrane.

Egg cell

haploid nucleus — cell membrane — ribosomes — cytoplasm — mitochondria

Sperm cell

acrosome — haploid nucleus — mitochondrion — tail

Ciliated epithelial cell

cilia — mitochondrion — ribosomes — cell membrane — cytoplasm — nucleus

---

Now try this

1 Give **one** similarity and **one** difference between a bacterial cell and an animal cell. **(2 marks)**

2 The diagram shows a root hair cell. Explain how the shape of this cell is related to its function. **(2 marks)**

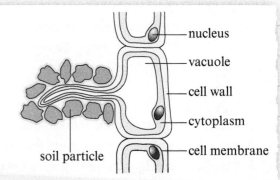

nucleus — vacuole — cell wall — cytoplasm — cell membrane

soil particle

A root hair cell in a plant absorbs minerals that have been dissolved in water.

Describe how the shape of the cell is different from other cells, and then give a reason why this is an advantage.

2

Microscopes and magnification

As microscope technology has developed over time, we have been able to see more of the **structures of cells** and to know more about the **role** of sub-cellular structures.

Using microscopes

Before microscopes were invented about 350 years ago, people could not see the cells in organisms. Magnification enables you to see plant cells, animal cells and bacterial cells, and the structures inside them.

A **light microscope** uses light to magnify objects. The greatest possible magnification using a light microscope is about ×2000.

An **electron microscope** uses electrons to view an object. This makes it possible to magnify objects up to about ×10 million. You can see objects in cells more clearly and in far more detail with an electron microscope than with a light microscope.

🖩 Maths skills **Calculating magnification**

$$\text{Magnification (M)} = \frac{\text{Image size (I)}}{\text{Real size (R)}}$$

✓ Measure image in millimetres (mm).

✓ Multiply by 1000 to get measurement in micrometres (μm).

✓ If the image has a scale bar, use that to find the answer.

Cover up the term you are trying to find to show the expression required to calculate it.

Worked example

1μm

Calculate the magnification of this image. **(2 marks)**

scale bar (image size, I) = 20 mm

20 × 10³ = 20 000 μm

so I = 20 000 μm

real size (R) = 1 μm (from diagram)

magnification = I ÷ R = 20 000 ÷ 1

magnification = ×20 000

Worked example

Some cells were viewed by microscope using a ×4 eyepiece and a ×20 objective. Calculate the magnification of the cells seen through the microscope (see page 5 for a diagram of a microscope). **(1 mark)**

Magnification of object

$= \begin{array}{c}\text{magnification}\\\text{of eyepiece}\end{array} \times \begin{array}{c}\text{magnification}\\\text{of objective}\end{array}$

= 4 × 20 = 80

The cells will be magnified 80 times by the microscope.

Always show your working in a calculation. Even if you get the answer wrong you may be able to show that you understand the method.

Now try this

A cell is viewed under a light microscope using a ×40 objective and a ×10 eyepiece.
(a) Calculate the total magnification. **(1 mark)**
(b) The image is 1.2 mm long. Use your answer to part (a) to calculate the actual length of the cell. **(1 mark)**

3

Dealing with numbers

Many structures in biology are very small so you will use very small **units of measurement**.

Describing small structures

Smaller structures need smaller units:

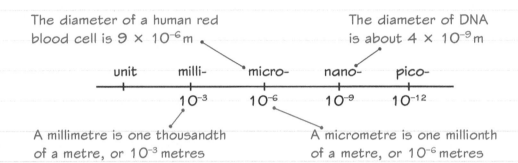

The diameter of a human red blood cell is 9×10^{-6} m

The diameter of DNA is about 4×10^{-9} m

unit	milli-	micro-	nano-	pico-
	10^{-3}	10^{-6}	10^{-9}	10^{-12}

A millimetre is one thousandth of a metre, or 10^{-3} metres

A micrometre is one millionth of a metre, or 10^{-6} metres

There are 1000 millimetres in a metre.

There are 1 000 000 micrometres in a metre.

There are 1 000 000 000 nanometres in a metre.

There are 1 000 000 000 000 picometres in a metre.

Also, notice that there are 1000 picometres in a nanometre, or 1000 micrometres in a millimetre.

Worked example

A mitochondrion is 0.002 mm long.
Give this length in:

(a) micrometres   **(1 mark)**

2 μm

(b) nanometres   **(1 mark)**

2000 nm

> Notice that there are 1000 nanometres in 1 micrometre.

Now try this

1 Match the structure to its correct average size.

Protein molecule	Chloroplast	Cell	
2 micrometres	10 nanometres	0.1 millimetres	**(2 marks)**

2 A human egg is 0.000 13 m long. State the length of the egg in micrometres. **(1 mark)**

3 The bacterial cell on page 3 is 2 μm long. Use this information to estimate the width of the cell. **(1 mark)**

Using a light microscope

 Practical skills You can use a **microscope** to **observe cells**. You can then produce accurate labelled diagrams from your observations (see page 6 for how to produce a labelled diagram).

Core practical

Using a light microscope safely
- Always start with the lowest **power objective** under the eyepiece.
- Clip the **slide** securely on the stage.
- Adjust the **light source (mirror)** so that light goes up through the slide.

If you use the Sun as a source of light, make sure the microscope mirror does not point directly at the Sun as this could permanently damage your eyesight.

- eyepiece
- objective
- coarse focusing wheel
- stage with clips to hold slide
- fine focusing wheel
- mirror to reflect light through slide

- Use the **coarse focusing wheel** to focus on the slide.
- Move the slide so that the cell you will draw is in the middle of the view.
- If needed, move a higher power objective into position above the slide.
- Use the **fine focusing wheel** to bring the cell back into focus.

Never use the coarse focusing wheel with a higher power objective, as it may crash into the slide.

If you cannot see the part of the slide you need with a higher power objective, go back to using the lower power objective to bring it back to centre view and to focus it before returning to the higher power objective.

Now try this

A student is given a microscope slide of a section through a leaf.
(a) Describe how the student should use a light microscope to study xylem cells in the leaf section.

(4 marks)

(b) The lens closest to the specimen is called the:
- ☐ **A** subjective
- ☐ **B** eyepiece
- ☐ **C** objective
- ☐ **D** stage

(1 mark)

Drawing labelled diagrams

🧪 **Practical skills** You can use a microscope to produce **accurate labelled diagrams** of cells and their structures (see page 5 for how to set up and use a light microscope).

Core practical

Aim

To produce a labelled diagram of a plant cell.

Apparatus

- light microscope
- unlined paper
- sharp HB pencil
- rubber
- ruler

Method

Focus the microscope on a single cell.

Carefully draw details of the parts that are important to your study. Other parts can be drawn just in outline.

Keep looking back at the specimen as you make the drawing, and only draw what you see, not what you think you ought to see.

Results

Pondweed cell ×650

chloroplast

cell walls of two neighbouring cells

cytoplasm and vacuole (not obvious)

nucleus

If a line is in the wrong place, rub it out cleanly before drawing it in the correct position. Your drawing should be as clear as possible.

Keep the relative sizes of structures approximately correct and label all the key parts of your drawing.

Labels should be outside the drawing and label lines must not cross.

Use a ruler to draw label lines to link labels to the correct parts of the drawing.

Never use shading.

Give your drawing a clear title saying what the specimen is, and always give the magnification, e.g. ×100. (See page 3 to help you calculate the magnification.)

Now try this

The photo shows some cells in a blood smear seen under a light microscope at ×1000.
Draw and label one example of each cell in the smear. **(3 marks)**

Enzymes

Enzymes are biological **catalysts** that control reactions in the body. Each enzyme is **specific** (only works with one substrate) to its substrate and the **activity** of enzymes is affected by temperature, substrate concentration and pH.

Effect of temperature and substrate concentration

At the **optimum temperature** the enzyme is working at its fastest rate.

Higher temperatures cause the active site to change shape, so it can't hold the substrate as tightly and the reaction goes more slowly.

Adding more substrate at this point has little effect because the active site of every enzyme molecule is working.

At lower temperatures, molecules move more slowly. So substrate molecules take longer to fit into and react in the active site.

At very high temperatures the active site breaks up and the enzyme is **denatured**.

At this point not every active site of each enzyme molecule is working, so adding more substrate increases the rate of reaction.

Worked example

The diagram shows an enzyme-controlled reaction.

two different substrate molecules

(a) State the name of the part labelled X. **(1 mark)**

product molecule

(b) Explain the role of the active site in an enzyme-controlled reaction. **(4 marks)**

The shape of the active site matches the shape of the substrate molecules and holds them close together so bonds can form between them to make the product. The product molecule doesn't fit the active site well so it is released from the enzyme.

The **substrate** fits like a 'key' into the **active site** (the 'lock'). Enzymes are specific because only a substrate with the right shape can fit the active site.

Worked example

Draw a graph of rate of reaction against pH for an enzyme with an optimum pH of 6. Label your graph to explain what you have drawn. **(2 marks)**

Changing the pH can change the shape of the enzyme's active site, and so change its ability to bond with the substrate.

The enzyme works fastest at the optimum pH.

As you go further from the optimum pH, the rate of reaction is slower as the enzyme gradually denatures.

Now try this

1 Explain what is meant by the active site of an enzyme. **(2 marks)**

2 Enzymes in the human body have an optimum temperature of about 37 °C. Explain why our body temperature is controlled to stay at about 37 °C. **(2 marks)**

pH and enzyme activity

 Practical skills You can **investigate the effect of pH on the rate on enzyme activity** by measuring the rate of an enzyme-controlled reaction at one pH, and comparing it with the rate at other pH values. You can revise enzymes on page 7.

Core practical

> Starch is broken down by amylase to sugars.

> Buffering the solution makes sure the pH doesn't change during the experiment.

> Keeping the solution at the optimum temperature for the enzyme is best.

> Iodine solution is usually yellow/orange. In the presence of starch, it turns blue/black.

Aim

To investigate the effect of pH on amylase activity.

Methods

- Add amylase to buffered starch solution in a test tube.
- Place the tube in a water bath heated by a Bunsen burner for a constant temperature.
- Take samples of the mixture at regular intervals (e.g. every 10 s) and mix them with a fresh drop of iodine solution on a dimple tile.
- Repeat the test until the iodine solution stops changing colour when the starch/amylase mixture is added. Record the time taken for this to happen.
- Repeat the procedure at different pH values.

Results

Record the values for each pH in a table. Then, you can draw a graph like the one given below.

Conclusion

The results show that the time taken for all the starch to be digested by the amylase decreases from pH 4 to pH 6, and then increases again. The optimum pH for this enzyme is pH 6.

Maths skills — Reaction rate

You can calculate the relative rate of reaction for a particular pH, as $\frac{1}{time}$ because the mass of starch used at each pH is the same. You can then compare the rates of reaction of amylase at different pHs. For this you do not have units.

For example: all starch was digested in 20 s at pH 6. The rate of reaction at pH 6 is $\frac{1}{20}$ = 0.05/s. However, this is not a true rate. For a true rate of reaction you would need to have the mass of starch digested by the enzyme divided by the time taken. The units for this would be g/s.

Method improvements

- Using more accurate measuring apparatus
- taking the mean of several repeats at each pH to help reduce the effect of random variation
- taking measurements over a narrower range of pH.

Now try this

1 (a) Calculate the relative rate of reaction of amylase at pH 9 in the core practical. **(1 mark)**
   (b) Explain why the graph shows that the optimum pH for this enzyme was pH 8. **(2 marks)**

2 A student repeated the experiment using solutions of pH 7.2, 7.6, 8.0, 8.4 and 8.8. Explain why the results of this experiment could produce a more accurate answer for the optimum pH of the enzyme. **(2 marks)**

The importance of enzymes

Enzymes are biological **catalysts** that control reactions in the body. They catalyse reactions that **synthesise** large molecules from smaller ones and **break down** large molecules into smaller ones.

Enzymes as catalysts

Enzymes **speed up** the rate of a chemical reaction but are not used up in the reaction. This means they can be used over and over again.

Make sure you remember at least some examples of enzymes and the reactions they catalyse.

Digestion and synthesis

Some enzymes **digest** large molecules into smaller molecules. This happens in the gut where large food molecules are broken down so that they can be absorbed into the blood.

| | digestion | | | digestion | | | digestion | |

Carbohydrates e.g. starch for energy storage in plants → (digestion amylase) → Sugars e.g. glucose for respiration → (synthesis) Lipids e.g. for energy storage → (digestion lipase) → Fatty acids and glycerol e.g. for respiration → (synthesis) Proteins e.g. for muscle cells → (digestion protease) → Amino acids e.g. to make enzymes → (synthesis)

Some enzymes **synthesise** larger molecules from smaller molecules. This is important inside cells for supporting life processes and growth.

Worked example

Complete the table.   **(3 marks)**

Large molecule	Smaller molecules it is broken down into
carbohydrates	sugars
proteins	amino acids
lipids	fatty acids and glycerol

Remember you need to mention **both** fatty acids **and** glycerol to get the mark.

Worked example

People with cystic fibrosis have thick mucus lining their gut. This stops enzymes being secreted into the gut. Explain why they need to take capsules containing enzymes before a meal.   **(3 marks)**

The thick mucus stops the body's own enzymes from entering the gut to digest the food. If people with cystic fibrosis didn't take enzyme capsules before meals, their food would not be digested into smaller, soluble molecules. As a result, they would not absorb enough nutrients.

Now try this

1 The enzyme that digests lipids will not digest proteins. Explain why.   **(2 marks)**

2 Name the part of a cell where you expect to find enzymes needed to make proteins (protein synthesis).   **(1 mark)**

Think about what you know about cell structure (see page 1 for the generalised structures of plant and animal cells).

Using reagents in food tests

Practical skills You can use chemical reagents to **identify starch, reducing sugars, proteins and fats in food**. Each food substance has its own tests.

Core practical

Aim

To investigate the use of chemical reagents to identify substances in food.

Apparatus

- test tubes
- water bath
- iodine solution
- Benedict's solution
- 0.1 mol dm^{-3} potassium hydroxide solution
- 0.01 mol dm^{-3} copper sulfate solution
- ethanol
- water
- food

Method

To test for starch: Place a few drops of iodine solution on solid food, or mix with a solution of the food.

To test for reducing sugars: Add an equal volume of Benedict's solution to a food solution and mix. Heat the mixture in a 95 °C water bath for a few minutes.

To test for proteins (biuret test): Add an equal volume of 0.1 mol dm^{-3} potassium hydroxide solution to the food solution and mix. Add a few drops of 0.01 mol dm^{-3} copper sulfate solution and mix.

To test for fats: Add an equal volume of ethanol to the food solution, and shake thoroughly. Add water to the mixture.

Results

Test reagent	Tests for ...	Colour of reagent/ negative result	Colour if food present
iodine solution	starch	yellow/orange	blue/black
Benedict's solution	reducing sugar	blue	green→orange→red (depending on how much sugar present)
biuret test	protein	pale blue	pale purple
ethanol	fat	clear	cloudy

Safety note:
- Handle iodine solution carefully as it can stain skin and clothing.
- Wear suitable eye protection for all these tests.
- Work safely with hot water, to avoid scalding. Use a heat-resistant glove or tongs to handle hot equipment.

Reducing sugars

These cause a reduction reaction with the reagent. They include sugars such as glucose and fructose, but not sucrose (table sugar).

Now try this

The table shows the results of food tests carried out on a food sample.
Identify the substances in the food. **(4 marks)**

Test reagent	Result
iodine solution	yellow/orange
Benedict's solution	green
biuret test	pale blue
ethanol	clear

Using calorimetry

You can find the **energy** in a sample of food using calorimetry.

1 The temperature of the water at the start is measured.

2 The mass of the food sample is measured.

3 The food is set alight (e.g. in a Bunsen flame), then placed immediately under the tube.

4 The temperature of the water at the end is measured, and the change in temperature is calculated.

The calorimeter contains a measured volume of water.

When all the food is burned, the increase in temperature is related to the energy released from the food.

thermometer — large test tube

— clamp stand

mounted needle

burning potato snack

— water

- The energy released from the food by burning is transferred to the water.
- As the water gains energy, its temperature increases.

Worked example

A student used calorimetry to measure the energy in a potato snack, using the apparatus shown above. The test tube contained 10 cm³ water. Give **two** reasons why this may not be an accurate measurement. **(2 marks)**

Taking too long to move the burning food to under the tube, or holding the food at different distances from the tube. This would affect how much energy is transferred to the surrounding air and not the tube.

You could give other reasons, such as not measuring the mass of food/initial temperature/volume of water accurately, or the food not burning completely. You may be able to think of others.

🧮 Maths skills — Calculating the energy in food

It takes 4.2 J of energy to raise the temperature of 1 cm³ of water by 1 °C. For example, the energy needed to raise the temperature of 20 cm³ of water by 18°C is:

20 × 4.2 × 18

= 1512 J

This is 1512/1000 = 1.512 kJ.

If 3 g of food was used to heat the water, the energy content of the food is:

1.512/3 = 0.504 kJ/g

So 125 g of the same food contains:

125 × 0.504 = 63 kJ of energy

Now try this

When 2 g of crisps are burned, 100 cm³ of water increases in temperature by 40 °C.

(a) Calculate the energy, in kJ, released by 2 g of crisps. **(1 mark)**

(b) Use your answer to part (a) to calculate the energy released by 1 g of crisps. **(1 mark)**

(c) Use your answer to part (b) to calculate the energy content of a 25 g bag of crisps. **(1 mark)**

Getting in and out of cells

Dissolved substances (**solutes**) move into and out of cells by **diffusion** and **active transport**. Water moves into and out of cells by **osmosis**.

Diffusion

high concentration of dissolved molecules (concentrated solution)

partially permeable membrane

More molecules move from the high concentration to the lower concentration than vice versa, so the net movement is **down** the concentration gradient.

low concentration of dissolved molecules (dilute solution)

Diffusion is important in the body, for example, to move oxygen into cells and to remove carbon dioxide.

Active transport

partially permeable membrane

Active transport needs energy from respiration.

low concentration of dissolved molecules (dilute solution)

high concentration of dissolved molecules (concentrated solution)

There is net movement against the concentration gradient.

Active transport makes it possible for cells to absorb ions from very dilute solutions, e.g. root cells absorb minerals from soil water, and small intestine cells absorb glucose from digested food in the gut into the body.

Worked example

The diagram shows the results of an experiment. At the start, the level of solution inside the tube and the level of water in the beaker were the same. Name the process that caused the change and explain what happened. **(3 marks)**

beaker

water

capillary tubing

thread

Visking tubing (partially permeable membrane)

30% sucrose solution

thread

The process is called osmosis. To start with there were more water molecules in the water than in the same volume of sucrose solution, so more water molecules crossed the membrane into the tubing than going the other way. So the level of solution in the capillary rose.

Osmosis is the name given to a special case of diffusion. Osmosis is the net movement of water molecules across a partially permeable membrane from a low solute concentration to a high solute concentration.

Now try this

1 Define **osmosis**. **(2 marks)**

2 (a) Give one similarity between diffusion and osmosis. **(1 mark)**
   (b) Give one difference between diffusion and active transport. **(1 mark)**

3 A plant root is treated with a poison that prevents respiration. Explain why the root cells still absorb water from a dilute solution, but cannot absorb mineral ions. **(4 marks)**

Remember that respiration provides the energy for active transport but there are other ways that substances can enter cells which do not require energy from respiration.

Osmosis in potatoes

 Practical skills You can investigate **osmosis** by calculating the change in mass of pieces of potato that have been placed in solutions of different solute concentration.

Core practical

Aim

To investigate osmosis using potatoes.

Apparatus

potato

- pieces of potato about $3 \times 1 \times 1$ cm
- boiling tubes
- accurate balance
- paper towels
- forceps
- solutions of different solute concentration (0, 0.2, 0.4, 0.6, 0.8, 1.0 mol dm^{-3})
- marker pen

Method

1. Mark the value of one solute concentration on one tube and repeat using a different tube for each concentration. Fill each tube two-thirds full of the appropriate solution.

2. Blot a piece of potato dry on a paper towel, then measure and record its mass. Use the forceps to place it into one of the tubes, and record the tube. Repeat for all tubes.

3. After 20 minutes, use the forceps to remove each piece of potato, blot it dry and measure its mass again. Record all final masses.

Results

The percentage change in mass of each potato slice is calculated and recorded, indicating whether mass was gained or lost.

Conclusion

The results show that when the solution concentration is very dilute, water enters the potato cells. This is due to osmosis because the solute concentration of the potato cells is greater than the surrounding solution. As the solute concentration of the solution increases above that inside the potato cells, osmosis causes water to be lost from the potato.

Remember, finding the percentage change in mass allows you to compare results from the different tubes, because the pieces of potato weren't all exactly the same mass to begin with.

Worked example

The initial mass of a potato slice was 16.52 g. After soaking in a solution the final mass was 20.15 g. Calculate the percentage change in mass.
(4 marks)

% change in mass =
$$\frac{\text{final mass} - \text{initial mass}}{\text{initial mass}} \times 100\% =$$
$$\frac{20.15 - 16.52}{16.52} \times 100 = 21.97\% \text{ gained}$$
(or +21.97%)

 The solute in the solutions must be something that is too large to diffuse across the cell membrane. Sucrose is often used.

The change in mass may be very small. You should measure to 2 d.p.

 Blotting removes surface water, and can help to increase the accuracy and repeatability of measurements.

Repeating the test at each solute concentration, and calculating the mean of the results, can help to reduce the effect of random variation.

Now try this

The table shows the results of an osmosis experiment using potato pieces.

(a) Calculate the percentage change in mass of potato at each concentration. **(2 marks)**

(b) Use your answers to estimate the solute concentration of the potato cells. Explain your answer. **(2 marks)**

Solution concentration (mol dm^{-3})	Initial mass (g)	Final mass (g)
0	16.52	20.15
0.2	15.90	16.70
0.4	17.06	15.69
0.6	16.88	14.36
0.8	16.23	12.32

13

Extended response – Key concepts

There will be one or more 6-mark questions on your exam paper. For these questions, you will need to think scientifically, and structure your answer logically showing how the points you make are related to each other. For the questions on this page, you can revise the topics on **enzyme activity** on pages 7 to 9.

Worked example

The graph shows the results of an experiment into the effect of temperature on the activity of the enzyme amylase on starch. Explain the results shown in the graph. **(6 marks)**

The graph shows that activity of the bacterial amylase increased from 30°C up to a maximum at 50°C, and then decreased as the temperature increased further to 70°C. The maximum activity is at the optimum temperature, which is about 50°C for this enzyme.

Enzyme activity increases with increasing temperature up to the optimum because particles move faster. Starch molecules fit into the active site of enzyme molecules more quickly and are broken down more quickly, releasing the active site for another starch molecule.

Beyond the optimum temperature, the shape of the active site starts to change, making it more difficult for the substrate to fit into it. So activity slows down. The active site shape changes more as temperature increases further, until the enzyme becomes denatured and stops being able to catalyse the reaction.

Before you explain the results, describe what the graph shows. Use values on the graph to add details to your answer. Remember to include important science words that are relevant in your answer.

Enzyme activity should be linked to how the active site of the enzyme and the substrate interact.

Make sure you explain each part of the graph clearly, linking your knowledge and understanding to give a good explanation of what is happening.

Command word: Explain

An **explain** question requires a reason for what is happening. Use a word such as 'because' to clearly link a description with its reason.

Now try this

The graph on the right shows the effect of starch concentration on the activity of a bacterial amylase. Explain the results shown in the graph. **(6 marks)**

Mitosis

There are two types of cell division, **mitosis** and meiosis. Mitosis is covered here; meiosis is covered on page 26.

Mitosis is a type of **cell division** that takes place in several stages. There are two types of **cell division**. **Mitosis** is the cell division that happens in body cells. A **body cell** is any cell except those that produce **gametes** (sex cells).

The cell that is dividing is called the **parent cell** and the two new cells that are formed are called **daughter cells**. The daughter cells are identical to the parent cell, so if the parent cell is diploid then the daughter cells will be diploid too. You should be clear about the differences between meiosis and mitosis.

Three things to remember

- ✓ Mi-to-sis makes two cells.
- ✓ MiTosis makes genetically idenTical cells.
- ✓ Diploid means Double (two sets of) chromosomes.

Stages of mitosis

Each chromosome consists of two chromatids. The nuclear membrane breaks down.

The chromatids separate and one chromatid from each pair is pulled to each pole of the cell. The chromatids can now be called chromosomes.

Finally, the cell splits into two. This is called **cytokinesis**.

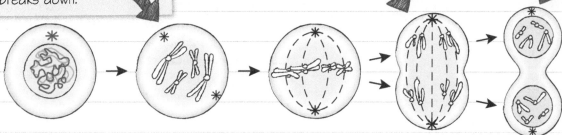

Interphase   Prophase   Metaphase   Anaphase   Telophase and cytokinesis

At the end of interphase, chromosomes start to become visible. The DNA has already been copied.

Chromosomes line up along the middle of the cell.

Spindle fibres disappear and a new nuclear membrane forms round each group of chromosomes during telophase.

Remember the stages of mitosis using the mnemonic IPMAT:
Interphase
Prophase
Metaphase
Anaphase
Telophase and cytokinesis

Worked example

(a) Body cells have two sets of chromosomes. Explain how this happens. **(2 marks)**

One set of chromosomes comes from the mother and one set comes from the father.

(b) Explain how the daughter cells are genetically identical. **(2 marks)**

Each chromosome is copied; one copy of each chromosome goes into each daughter cell.

Interphase

A cell is in interphase most of the time.

Now try this

A cell divides by mitosis. Describe the daughter cells. **(2 marks)**

Cell growth and differentiation

Mitosis is used for growth, repair and asexual reproduction. After growth, cells can then **differentiate** into specialised cells. Growth and differentiation happen in different ways in plants and animals.

When does mitosis happen?

Normally cells only divide by mitosis when new diploid cells are needed for:
- growth
- repair (replacement of damaged cells)
- asexual reproduction.

Uncontrolled cell division

Cancer cells are abnormal cells that divide uncontrollably by mitosis to form a **tumour**.

Cells usually stop dividing when growth has finished, except when repair is needed. Sometimes the controls that tell cells when to stop dividing go wrong which leads to cancer.

Worked example

Aphids are insects that are pests of crop plants. In the summer they reproduce rapidly by asexual reproduction. Will the offspring of a single aphid be varied? Explain your answer. **(3 marks)**

The offspring will be produced by mitosis, so they will all be genetically identical to the parent aphid. They will all be diploid like the parent aphid.

Mitosis is used for asexual reproduction. This also occurs in plants, for example, when plants reproduce using bulbs or runners.

Growth in animals

In **animals**, a fertilised egg, or zygote, divides by mitosis to produce genetically identical daughter cells. These cells grow and divide by mitosis, and eventually **differentiate** into different types of cells to make up a whole organism. Differentiation creates **specialised cells** adapted to carry out a particular function. Examples of specialised animal cells include:
- red blood cells
- egg and sperm cells
- nerve cells
- bone cells
- smooth muscle cells.

Growth in plants

Plant cells divide by mitosis, just behind the tips of shoots and roots. After this the cells grow by enlarging. Young cells have small vacuoles which take in water by osmosis and enlarge, causing the cells to **elongate**. These cells can differentiate into specialised cell types. Most plant cells can **continue** to grow and differentiate throughout life.

Examples of specialised plant cells include:
- xylem
- phloem
- mesophyll cells
- root hair cells
- stoma cells.

leaf

shoot tip

area where cells are dividing rapidly to make more new cells

zone of **elongation**

differentiation of cells to form xylem and phloem

Now try this

 1 Some drugs stop mitosis. Explain why they are used to treat cancer. **(2 marks)**

 2 State what is meant by a specialised cell. **(1 mark)**

 3 Explain why cell differentiation is important. **(2 marks)**

Growth and percentile charts

When organisms **grow** they get bigger. Growth can be measured in different ways.

Estimating growth

Growth is a **permanent** increase in size. For example, a balloon that is blown up a little more has not 'grown' in size.

Percentile charts

Percentile charts can help to show if a child is growing faster or slower than is normal for their age.

Babies with a mass above the 95th line or below the 5th line may not be growing properly.

A baby whose mass decreases by two or more percentiles over their first year may not be growing normally.

The mass of a baby is measured regularly and compared with the chart.

95% of babies have a mass less than this

5% of babies have a mass less than this

Percentiles
— 5th
— 10th
— 25th
— 50th
— 75th
— 90th
— 95th

This chart is for baby girls. The chart for baby boys is similar, but they grow at a slightly different rate to girls.

Worked example

Look at the percentile chart. The crosses mark the mass of a baby girl measured each month.

(a) State the percentile that she belonged to in her first month. **(1 mark)**

75th percentile

(b) Do you think there was concern about this baby's mass increase in her first year? Explain your answer. **(2 marks)**

No, because her mass varied only between the 75th and 50th percentiles, and this amount of variation is normal.

Worked example

BMI is a measure of a healthy body mass. The government has produced percentile charts for BMI in children. A child has a clinically healthy weight if their BMI is between the 2nd and 91st percentile. A parent has been told that her son is on the 70th centile for BMI. Explain to her what this means. **(2 marks)**

This means the child has a higher BMI than 70% of children and a lower BMI than 30% of children. Because this falls between the 2nd and 91st percentile, the child has a clinically healthy weight.

Now try this

1 Describe one way in which you could measure the growth of a plant. **(2 marks)**

2 Describe what a percentile chart is used for. **(2 marks)**

3 Explain why an increase in the size of a balloon is not an example of growth but an increase in the size of a child is. **(2 marks)**

Stem cells

Stem cells have different functions in plants and animals. In humans, they have many potential uses in medicine.

What are stem cells?

Cells in an embryo are unspecialised. They divide to produce all the **specialised cells** in the body, such as neurones and muscle cells. Once the cells have differentiated they cannot divide to produce other kinds of cell.

Stem cells are cells that can divide to produce many types of cell. There are three kinds of stem cell:
- **Embryonic stem cells** are taken from embryos at a very early stage of division (e.g. 8 cells).
- **Adult stem cells** are found in differentiated tissue, such as bone or skin – they divide to replace damaged cells.
- Plants have **meristems** that are found in rapidly growing parts of the plant, e.g. tips of roots and shoots. These cells can divide to produce any kind of plant cell.

Embryonic stem cells

Embryonic stem cells have many uses, including:
- replacing or repairing brain cells to treat people with Parkinson's disease
- replacing damaged cells in the retina of the eye to treat some kinds of blindness
- growing new tissues in the lab to use for transplants or drug testing.

Adult stem cells

Adult stem cells (from bone marrow) can only form a limited number of cell types. They can be used for:
- treatment of leukaemia
- potentially growing new tissues that are genetically matched to the patient.

Using stem cells

embryonic stem cells

✓ easy to extract from embryo

✓ produce any type of cell

✗ embryo destroyed when cells removed – some people think embryos have a right to life

all stem cells

✓ replace faulty cell with healthy cell, so person is well again

! stem cells may not stop dividing, and so cause cancer

adult stem cells

✓ no embryo destroyed so not an ethical issue

✓ if taken from the person to be treated, will not cause rejection by the body

✗ produce only a few types of cell

✓ – Advantage   ✗ – Disadvantage   ! – Risk

Now try this

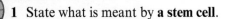

1 State what is meant by **a stem cell**.
(2 marks)

2 When gardeners cut off the top of a plant, the plant usually continues to grow sideways but does not grow taller. Explain why. (2 marks)

3 Explain **two** disadvantages of research into embryonic stem cells. (2 marks)

4 (a) State why embryonic stem cells could be more useful than adult stem cells to replace faulty cells. (1 mark)

(b) Describe **one** practical advantage of using adult stem cells from the patient instead of embryonic stem cells to replace faulty cells. (2 marks)

If an exam question asks for **two** advantages or disadvantages, make sure you give two **different** examples.

The brain and spinal cord

The brain and the spinal cord make up the **central nervous system**.

Parts of the brain

The cerebral hemispheres control **voluntary movement**, **interpret** sensory information and are responsible for **learning** and **memory**.

cerebral hemispheres

The cerebellum coordinates and controls precise and smooth **movement**.

The medulla oblongata regulates the **heart beat** and **breathing**.

medulla oblongata

cerebellum

The brain and spinal cord

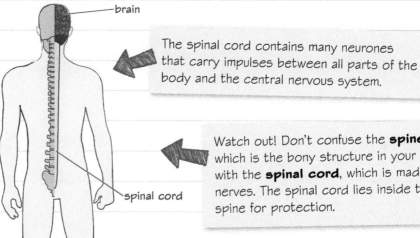

brain

The spinal cord contains many neurones that carry impulses between all parts of the body and the central nervous system.

Watch out! Don't confuse the **spine**, which is the bony structure in your back, with the **spinal cord**, which is made of nerves. The spinal cord lies inside the spine for protection.

spinal cord

Worked example

A person who has broken their spinal cord is paralysed from the point of the damage downwards. This means they cannot feel anything from the lower part of their body or move it. Explain why. **(2 marks)**

Nerve impulses to and from the lower part of the body pass through the spinal cord. If these nerves are damaged there is no way that impulses can be sent between the brain and the lower part of the body.

To answer this question fully, you will need to describe both the **role** of the spinal cord and the **effect** of damage to it.

Now try this

Complete the table to show the part of the brain responsible for each activity.
(2 marks)

Part of brain	Activity
	increasing heart rate during exercise
	reading a book
	balancing on a skate board
	recognising a person from a photograph

19

Neurones

Stimuli are detected by sensory **receptors** that send impulses along sensory **neurones** to the central nervous system. Neurones are specialised cells that carry nervous impulses.

Types of neurones

There are three main types of neurones. **Sensory neurones** carry impulses to the central nervous system. **Motor neurones** carry impulses from the central nervous system to effector organs. **Relay neurones** are found only in the central nervous system.

Sensory neurone

skin receptor cells — direction of impulse — cell body

Axon endings pass impulses to other neurones.

dendron — **axon** — fatty **myelin sheath**

Dendrites collect impulses from receptor cells.

carries impulses towards cell body

carries impulses away from cell body

insulates the neurone

Relay neurone

This carries impulse from one part of the central nervous system to another.

Motor neurone

The electrical impulse jumps from one gap in the myelin sheath to the next, speeding up the rate of transmission.

The nerve ending transmits the impulse to an effector, such as a muscle or gland.

nerve ending — **myelin sheath** — **axon** — nucleus — dendrite — cytoplasm — cell membrane

The electrical impulse cannot cross the fatty myelin sheath.

The axon carries the electrical impulse over long distances through the body.

Worked example

Complete the table with the name of the structure that corresponds to each function listed. **(3 marks)**

Structure	Function
axon	carries impulses away from the cell body
dendrite	receiving impulses from receptor cells and other neurones
myelin sheath	a fatty layer that provides electrical insulation around the neurone

Now try this

1 Give the roles of sensory, motor and relay neurones in the nervous system. **(3 marks)**
2 Explain how the structure of a sensory neurone is related to its function. **(2 marks)**

Responding to stimuli

Sensory neurones **carry impulses** from receptors to the central nervous system.

Synapses

The point where two neurones meet is called a **synapse**. There is a small gap between the neurones. The electrical nerve impulse cannot cross this gap, and the impulse is carried by **neurotransmitters**.

1 Electrical nerve impulse reaches end of axon.

synapse

2 Electrical impulse causes chemical neurotransmitter to be released from vesicles in the neurone into the gap between the neurones.

3 Neurotransmitter diffuses across the gap and fits into receptors, causing a new electrical impulse in the next neurone.

Worked example

Explain the role of a neurotransmitter. **(2 marks)**

It is a chemical released from one neurone that carries the impulse across the synaptic gap to the next neurone. Without it, the electrical impulse cannot cross the synaptic gap.

Stimulus detected by receptor

Impulses pass along sensory neurone to spinal cord

Impulses pass to relay neurone

Impulses pass from relay neurone to motor neurone

Impulses pass along motor neurone to effector, in this case a muscle

Hand moves away from stimulus

The reflex arc

sensory neurone

spinal cord

motor neurone

relay neurone

biceps muscle

heat receptor in the skin

Reflex arcs involve only three neurones, and impulses pass to and from the spinal cord. This provides a fast response that does not involve the brain. Reflex arcs are:
- immediate (happens very fast)
- involuntary (the brain isn't needed)
- innate (not learned)
- invariable (always exactly the same).

These reflexes help protect us from immediate harm, such as the eye blink reflex which protects the eye if something comes close to it.

If the impulses had to go to the brain to be processed, there would be many more synapses, so the response would take longer.

Now try this

1 A person's finger gets pricked by a pin and the person removes their finger rapidly. Describe how the reflex arc causes this. **(4 marks)**

2 Describe how impulses can pass across a synapse. **(3 marks)**

The eye

The eye is a **sensory receptor** that detects light and sends electrical impulses along sensory neurones to the brain.

Parts of the eye

suspensory ligaments
iris
lens
pupil
cornea
ciliary muscles
retina
optic nerve

Light enters the eye through a hole called the pupil. The **cornea** and the **lens** focus the light to form a sharp image on the **retina**. The retina contains special receptor cells called rods and cones that detect the light and form an image. The nerves in the retina convert the image into electrical signals that are sent to the brain along the optic nerve.

Focusing the image

The eye lens changes shape to produce a sharp image on the retina.

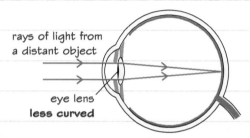

rays of light from a distant object
eye lens **less curved**

rays of light from a near object
eye lens **more curved**

Object	Ciliary muscles	Suspensory ligaments	Shape of lens
near	contracted	slack	fat and rounded
far	relaxed	tight	thin and flattened

Explain the role of the two different kinds of receptor cells in the retina. **(2 marks)**

Cone cells are sensitive to bright light and respond to different colours. Rod cells are sensitive at low light intensity and respond only to how dark or light something is.

> You are asked for the two different kinds of cells so name both, then give the role for each.

The iris

In bright light the circular muscles in the iris contract to make the pupil smaller.

In dim light the radial muscles contract to make the pupil larger.

The **iris** is a ring of muscle that controls the size of the pupil. It does this to protect the rods and cones in bright light and to let more light in when light is dim.

Now try this

1 (a) Which part of the eye is an opening that allows light to enter the eye?

☐ **A** iris ☐ **B** pupil

☐ **C** cornea ☐ **D** retina **(1 mark)**

(b) Which is the coloured part around the opening in part (a)?

☐ **A** iris ☐ **B** pupil

☐ **C** rods ☐ **D** retina **(1 mark)**

2 Explain why it is difficult to detect the colour of cars driving along a road at night. **(2 marks)**

3 Describe the function of the cornea and lens. **(2 marks)**

Eye problems

Problems with the eye include **colour blindness**, **long-** or **short-sightedness**, and **cataracts**. Some of these can be corrected with lenses.

Cataracts

Cataracts occur when the lens becomes cloudy, so light cannot pass through it properly. The person receives a blurred image on the retina. Cataracts can be treated by replacing the cloudy lens with a clear **artificial lens**.

Colour blindness

A normal retina contains three types of **cone** that detect red, green and blue light. The colour of an image is detected by how much each type of cone is stimulated. **Colour blindness** occurs when at least one type of cone is missing or does not work properly. This inherited disorder occurs mostly in males. In **red–green colour blindness**, either red or green cones are missing, and the person cannot distinguish between the colours red and green.

Long sight

Long-sighted people can focus on distant objects but not near ones. This can be corrected using spectacles with **converging** lenses.

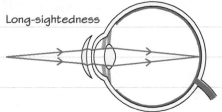

Long-sightedness

A **converging** lens brings the rays together so light is focused on the retina.

Short sight

Short-sighted people can focus on close objects but not distant ones. This can be corrected using spectacles with **diverging** lenses.

Short-sightedness

A **diverging** lens makes the rays come together further away, so light is focused on the retina.

> Long and short sight can also be corrected with laser surgery and with contact lenses that work with the eye's own lens to adjust the path of the light through the eye.

Worked example

What are the causes and symptoms of
(a) short sight **(2 marks)**
(b) long sight? **(2 marks)**

(a) A short-sighted person may have eyeballs that are too long, or eye lenses that are too powerful even when the muscles are relaxed. A person with short sight can focus on close objects but not distant ones.

(b) A long-sighted person may have eyeballs that are too short, or eye lenses that are not powerful enough. This often happens as we get older and the lens does not bend enough. A person with long sight can focus on distant objects but not close ones.

Now try this

1 Suggest how a normal eye detects the colour white. **(1 mark)**

2 Suggest how the eye can detect the colour yellow. **(2 marks)**

3 Explain why people with cataracts have a blurred image on the retina. **(2 marks)**

Extended response – Cells and control

There will be one or more 6-mark questions on your exam paper. For these questions, you will need to think scientifically and structure your answer logically, showing how the points you make are related to each other. You can revise the topic for this question, which is about **neurones** and **responding to stimuli**, on pages 20 and 21.

Worked example

Motor neurones are one type of cell found in the nervous system. The diagram shows the structure of a motor neurone.

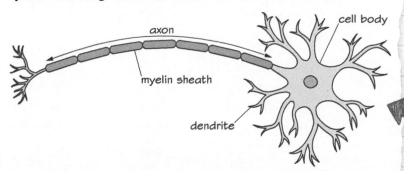

Explain how the structure of a motor neurone is related to its function. **(6 marks)**

Neurones carry nervous impulses along their axons. Motor neurones carry impulses from relay neurones to effectors such as muscles or glands. They have long axons to carry impulses long distances through the body. The myelin sheath insulates the axon, making the impulses travel faster.

Motor neurones have many tiny dendrites at the end of the axon. These receive impulses from other neurones in the nervous system, connecting neurones together.

The gap between one neurone and the next is called a synapse. Chemicals released into the synapse allow the signal to pass to the next neurone.

Command word: Explain

When you are asked to **explain** something, it is not enough just to state or describe it.

Your answer **must** contain some reasoning or justification of the points you make.

> Diagrams are shown in questions to give you information that will be useful in your answers. Make sure you study them carefully.

> The question does not ask for the function of motor neurones, but the answer includes the function. This is important for explaining how the structure and function are related.

> The answer mentions nervous impulses, but they could be called signals or messages instead.

> This part of the answer includes a description of the synapse. It is not part of the cell itself, but an understanding of the synapse is needed to fully explain the function of a motor neurone.

> You need to show comprehensive knowledge and understanding, using relevant scientific ideas, to support your explanations. In this answer, the structure of the three main parts of the motor neurone are described and explained (the axon, myelin sheath and dendrites).

Now try this

When a bright light shines into the eye, muscles in the iris contract. The size of the pupil decreases so that less light can enter the eye. This is an example of a reflex. Describe how impulses travel through the reflex arc involved, starting with receptor cells in the eye.

(6 marks)

> Think about the route, including the three types of neurones involved and the effector. Link your statements in a sensible order.

Asexual and sexual reproduction

Reproduction is the production of new individuals. There are two forms of reproduction. Each has advantages and disadvantages.

① Sexual reproduction

gamete from mother fuses (joins) with gamete from father

⬇

mixes genetic information from each parent

⬇

offspring have different combinations of genes, so show variety in characteristics

Advantages

👍 Offspring are genetically different to parents and each other, so there is **variation**. This means that if the environment changes, then some individuals may survive.

Disadvantages

👎 The organism has to **find** a mate to reproduce, which takes time and energy.

② Asexual reproduction

no fusion of gametes – only one parent

⬇

no mixing of genetic information

⬇

all offspring have same genes as parent and each other

Advantages

👍 Only one parent – no need to find a mate and reproductive cycle is **faster**.

👍 Offspring are **genetically identical** to each other and to the parent. This is an advantage in organisms that are very well adapted to an unchanging environment. If the parent is well adapted to the environment, then the offspring will be too.

Disadvantages

👎 All offspring are genetically identical, so there is **no variation** in the population and if the environment changes then all may die.

Worked example

> It isn't enough to say mitosis – you need to say that this gives genetically identical cells.

(a) Describe how asexual reproduction produces genetically identical offspring. **(1 mark)**

This involves mitosis, which produces genetically identical cells.

(b) Aphids are insects that are pests of crop plants. They reproduce asexually in the summer but by sexual reproduction in the autumn. Explain the advantage to aphids of having both sexual and asexual reproduction. **(2 marks)**

Asexual reproduction in the summer means they produce lots of offspring very quickly while there is plenty of food available. In the autumn, they reproduce sexually so that the offspring show variation. This means that at least some of the offspring are likely to survive if the environment is harsh.

Now try this

1 Which of these is a disadvantage of sexual reproduction?

☐ **A** Only one parent
☐ **B** Organism needs to find a mate
☐ **C** Offspring genetically identical
☐ **D** Offspring show variation   **(1 mark)**

2 The offspring produced by asexual reproduction have the same genes as the parent and each other. Describe **one** way in which this is an advantage and **one** way in which it is a disadvantage. **(2 marks)**

Meiosis

Meiosis is a type of cell division that produces four **daughter cells**, each with half the number of chromosomes. Meiosis only happens in gamete-producing cells, producing genetically different **haploid** gametes. The other type of cell division, **mitosis**, is covered on page 15.

Stages of meiosis

The parent cell is a diploid cell. So it has two sets of chromosomes.

the other set of chromosomes

one set of chromosomes

pair of chromosomes

Before the parent cell divides, each chromosome is copied.

The parent cell divides in two and then in two again. Four daughter cells are produced.

Each daughter cell gets a copy of one chromosome from each pair.

Each daughter cell has only one set of chromosomes. So these are **haploid** cells. The daughter cells are not all identical – meiosis results in variation.

Remember: haploid cells, produced by meiosis (me-1-osis), have 1 set of chromosomes.

The cells produced by division are always called 'daughter cells', even if they will eventually turn into sperm cells.

Worked example

Give four differences between mitosis and meiosis.

(4 marks)

Meiosis produces four daughter cells, but mitosis only produces two.

Meiosis produces genetically different daughter cells, but in mitosis the daughter cells are identical to each other and to the parent cell.

Meiosis produces haploid cells, but mitosis produces diploid cells.

Mitosis occurs in body cells, but meiosis occurs only in gamete-producing cells.

Be careful to spell mitosis and meiosis correctly. If you write something like 'meitosis' or 'miosis' it won't be clear which kind of cell division you are referring to.

Now try this

1 Describe the outcome of meiosis of a diploid parent cell. **(3 marks)**
2 Explain the importance of meiosis. **(2 marks)**

You need to say enough for 2 marks here. It may help to think about what would happen if gametes were produced by mitosis and not meiosis.

3 In terms of the number of sets of chromosomes, describe the difference between haploid and diploid. **(2 marks)**
4 The cells produced by meiosis are
☐ **A** diploid
☐ **B** genetically different
☐ **C** embryos
☐ **D** identical **(1 mark)**

DNA

DNA is the **genetic material** found in the chromosomes in the nuclei of cells.

DNA in the cell

The nucleus contains chromosomes.

Most cells have a nucleus.

cell

chromosome

A chromosome consists of a string of genes.

A **gene** is a short piece of **DNA** that codes for a specific **protein**. You have genes for hair structure, eye colour, enzymes and every other protein in your body.

DNA

Each gene is a length of DNA. DNA is a long, coiled molecule formed from two strands. The strands are twisted in a **double helix**.

G ═ C
A ═ T
C ═ G
A ═ T
T ═ A

The two strands of the double helix are joined by pairs of **bases**. There are four different bases in DNA:
A = adenine   T = thymine
C = cytosine   G = guanine

Bases form **complementary pairs**:
A always pairs with T
C always pairs with G

Remember: straight A with straight T; curly C with curly G.

Weak hydrogen bonds between the base pairs hold the DNA strands together.

The **genome** is all the DNA in an organism.

DNA structure

DNA is a **polymer** made of many **monomers**, called **nucleotides**, joined together.

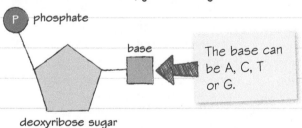

P phosphate

base

The base can be A, C, T or G.

deoxyribose sugar

🧪 Practical skills DNA from fruit

DNA can be extracted from fruit by:

1 grinding the fruit with sand, using a pestle and mortar, to separate the cells

2 adding a detergent to break open the membranes

3 adding ice-cold alcohol so that the DNA precipitates out.

Now try this

You do not need to know the names of the bases. You just need to know their letters are A, C, T and G.

1 Write a sentence to define each of these words:
   (a) gene   (b) genome.   **(2 marks)**

2 The sequence of bases on one strand of DNA is CGAT. Write down the sequence of bases on the complementary strand, and explain how you worked out your answer.   **(2 marks)**

3 Describe the structure of DNA.   **(4 marks)**

This question has 4 marks, so the answer needs 4 different ideas.

27

Gregor Mendel

Gregor Mendel was an Austrian monk who studied genetics. He was the first person to discover the basics of **inheritance**.

Mendel's experiment

Mendel cross-bred peas to determine which traits were **dominant** and which traits were **recessive**.

So although the trait for tall peas was dominant, the first generation of offspring still retained some information about the trait for dwarf peas. Mendel had discovered the basics of inheritance.

| **pure-bred peas** Mendel created **pure-bred** peas to use in his experiments. These would always produce identical offspring when bred with a pea of the same type. | → | **1st generation** He crossed pure-bred **dwarf peas** with pure-bred **tall peas** and discovered that all the offspring were tall. The trait for tall peas was **dominant** and the trait for dwarf peas was **recessive**. | → | **2nd generation** Mendel then removed the pure-bred peas and cross-bred the offspring with themselves. In the **second generation** about **one quarter** of the offspring were dwarf peas. |

Mendel's work is important because he set up his experiments scientifically.

He used peas because his earlier work showed a repeatable pattern of results.

He developed pure-breeding lines of peas to use in his experiments.

These produced offspring that were all identical to the parent for that particular trait. This meant he could repeat the experiments and know that he would get similar results each time.

He pollinated each plant by hand, so he knew which plants had been crossed.

He repeated his experiments many times, and kept detailed notes of his results.

Worked example

(a) Mendel crossed a pure-breeding tall pea with a pure-breeding dwarf pea. He obtained 128 offspring and they were all tall. Explain why Mendel had to prepare pure-breeding tall and dwarf plants before he started his experiment. **(3 marks)**

This was so that he knew the tall plants were all genetically the same and that the dwarf plants were also genetically the same. It meant he could repeat his results.

(b) He bred the offspring together and got 3980 tall and 1302 dwarf plants. Explain what Mendel could conclude from these results. **(3 marks)**

There was a factor for tallness that was dominant over the factor for dwarfness, because although there were no dwarf plants after the first cross, some dwarf plants appeared in the second generation.

Before Mendel

At the time Mendel was working, nobody knew about DNA, genes or chromosomes. Many people thought that offspring resulted from a 'blending' of the parents' characteristics.

Another idea, common at the time, was that sperm cells carried a miniature but perfectly formed offspring, and the female's egg provided an 'essence' that allowed the offspring to grow.

You need to state a conclusion and give a reason why the results support this conclusion.

Now try this

1 Mendel knew that tall was dominant and dwarfness was recessive in peas. Explain how. **(2 marks)**
2 Explain why Mendel carried out each of his crosses many times. **(1 mark)**

Genetic terms

You need to be able to explain all of the **genetic terms** in bold on this page.

Inside a cell

When **gametes** fuse at fertilisation, they form a diploid **zygote**. Each zygote inherits different alleles (genetic variants) of their genes from their parents. This produces variation in inherited characteristics between different individuals.

cell

Most cells contain a **nucleus** in which there are **chromosomes**.

There are two copies of each **chromosome** in body cells – each copy has the same genes in the same order along its length (except chromosomes that determine sex).

A **gene** is a short piece of DNA at a particular point on a chromosome – a gene codes for a characteristic, e.g. eye colour.

A gene may come in different forms, called **alleles**, that produce different variations of the characteristic, e.g. different eye colours.

Alleles

different alleles of the same gene – the person is **heterozygous** for this gene

Chromosomes of the same pair have the same genes in the same order.

these genes have the same allele on both chromosomes – the person is **homozygous** for these genes

Genetic definitions

The gene for coat colour in rabbits has different alleles. The allele for brown colour (B) is dominant over the allele for black colour (b). The table shows all the possible genotypes and phenotypes for these alleles.

Genotype shows the alleles (forms of the genes) in the individual. Remember that each body cell has two alleles for each characteristic – either two alleles that are the same or two that are different.

Genotype	Phenotype
BB	brown coat
Bb	brown coat
bb	black coat

Phenotype means the characteristics that are produced, including what the individual looks like.

The effect of the **dominant** allele will show when at least one copy is present in the genotype.

The effect of the **recessive** allele will only show when two copies are present in the genotype.

Now try this

Make sure you know the difference between a gene and an allele. This is a common mistake that students make.

1　Define the terms **chromosome**, **gene** and **allele**. **(3 marks)**

2　A pea plant has a recessive allele for white flower colour and a dominant allele for purple flower colour.
　(a) Identify if the plant is homozygous or heterozygous for flower colour, and explain your answer.
　　　(2 marks)
　(b) State the phenotype of the plant for flower colour. Explain your answer. **(2 marks)**

Monohybrid inheritance

Monohybrid inheritance can be explained using **genetic diagrams** and **Punnett squares**.

Genetic diagrams

Body cells contain two alleles for each gene. In this example, both parent plants are heterozygous – they have one allele for purple flower colour and one allele for white flower colour.

parent plants

pollen grains   egg cells

Purple colour is dominant (R). White colour is recessive (r).

different possible gametes

Half the gametes contain one allele. The other half contain the other allele.

possible combinations

genotype

phenotype

Worked example

Green seed pod (G) is dominant to yellow seed pod (g). Complete the Punnett square to show the possible offspring for plants heterozygous for seed pod colour, and calculate the (a) ratio, (b) probability and (c) percentage of possible offspring genotypes and phenotypes. **(4 marks)**

		parent genotype Gg	
	parent gametes	G	g
parent genotype Gg	G	GG green	Gg green
	g	Gg green	gg yellow

(a) Genotype 1 GG : 2 Gg : 1 gg
   Phenotype 3 green : 1 yellow

(b) Genotype 1/4 (1 out of 4) GG, 2/4 (1/2) Gg, and 1/4 gg
   Phenotype 3/4 green and 1/4 yellow

(c) Genotype 25% GG, 50% Gg, 25% gg
   Phenotype 75% green and 25% yellow

A **Punnett square** is a different way of showing the same information about how genotype is inherited and what effect this has on the phenotype.

Genetic diagrams and Punnett squares only show **possible** offspring, not the **actual** offspring from these parents.

Now try this

The allele for brown fur in rabbits is dominant. The allele for black fur is recessive. A heterozygous brown rabbit was bred with a homozygous black rabbit.
Use a diagram to show why half the baby rabbits should be brown.
(3 marks)

Remember to use a Punnett square when answering this question.

Family pedigrees

Cystic fibrosis (CF) is a genetic condition caused by a recessive allele. **Pedigree analysis** can be used to study the inheritance of dominant and recessive alleles.

Family pedigree showing inheritance of cystic fibrosis

You can use a **family pedigree** to show the inheritance of a genetic condition within a family, and to **predict** the chance that someone will inherit the faulty allele.

In the family pedigree below, both Ethan and Mia have CF. Ethan inherited his alleles from Arun and Beth. But they don't have the disease, so they must both be **carriers** (have one copy of the faulty allele).

Three generations are shown in this pedigree. Arun and Beth are the oldest generation.

Ethan and Mia must have two copies of the recessive allele, as they have the disease.

Worked example

The ability to taste phenylthiocarbamide (PTC) is a dominant condition. The diagram shows the inheritance of PTC tasting in one family. Describe the evidence that PTC tasting is controlled by a dominant allele.

(2 marks)

1 and 2 are both PTC tasters but they have two children who are non-tasters. Therefore PTC tasting must be dominant and non-tasting is recessive.

You are asked for **evidence** so make sure you refer to **specific individuals** in the pedigree.

Maths skills Pedigree analysis

Look at the family pedigree above. You can calculate the **probability** of Gill and Harry having a third child with cystic fibrosis using a Punnett square.

Mia has the disease, so Harry and Gill must both have one copy of the faulty allele.

There is one outcome (ff) that would lead to a child having CF, and three that would not:

P(third child has CF) = $\frac{1}{4}$ or 25%

There is more about Punnett squares on page 32.

Now try this

Look at the family pedigree in the worked example above.
(a) Give the genotype of individual 2. **(1 mark)**
(b) Individuals 9 and 10 have a fifth child. Calculate the probability that the child will be a PTC taster. **(2 marks)**

Remember that the trait is **dominant** so each person only needs **one copy** of the allele in order to be a PTC taster.

Sex determination

The sex of humans is determined at fertilisation and can be expressed using **genetic diagrams** and **Punnett squares**.

Sex chromosomes

The sex of humans is controlled by one pair of **sex chromosomes**. The genotype **XX** produces the **female** phenotype. The genotype **XY** produces the **male** phenotype.

Genotype and phenotype

The genotype is all the genes of the individual. The phenotype is what the individual looks like.

Worked example

Explain the proportions of the different sex chromosomes in the gametes of men and women. **(3 marks)**

Gametes are haploid because they are produced by meiosis. As the sex chromosomes in a woman's diploid body cell are both X, all the eggs she produces will contain one X chromosome. The sex chromosomes in a man's diploid body cells are XY, so 50% of his sperm will contain one X chromosome and the other 50% will contain one Y chromosome.

Genetic diagrams and Punnett squares

We can use a **genetic diagram** or **Punnett square** to show that the sex of an individual is determined at fertilisation.

Genetic diagram

parent's phenotype	male	female
parent's genotype	XY	XX
gametes	X Y	X X
possible offspring	XX XY XX XY	

Punnett square

		possible female gametes	
		X	X
possible male gametes	X	XX female	XX female
	Y	XY male	XY male

You can usually use either a Punnett square or a genetic diagram to answer a question about inheritance. Use the one that works best for you.

Both diagrams show that, at fertilisation, there is an equal chance of producing a male or a female:
• 50% male XY: 50% female XX
• ratio of 1 : 1 male : female
• 1 out of 2 chance of either male or female.

Use a Punnett square like this.

Now try this

1 At which of the following stages is the sex of a baby determined?

☐ **A** when the egg is fertilised
☐ **B** as the foetus develops in the womb
☐ **C** when the baby is born   **(1 mark)**

2 A couple have two sons. The woman is pregnant with another child. Draw a genetic diagram to show the % chance of this child being a girl.
(4 marks)

3 Explain why human eggs all contain one X chromosome.   **(2 marks)**

Inherited characteristics

The human ABO blood group is an example of an inherited characteristic controlled by a single gene that has **multiple alleles**.

Blood groups

There are four ABO blood groups controlled by three different alleles:

Phenotype (blood group)	Genotype
A	$I^A I^A$ or $I^A I^O$
B	$I^B I^B$ or $I^B I^O$
AB	$I^A I^B$
O	$I^O I^O$

- I stands for the blood group gene. The superscript shows the allele of that gene. There are other naming systems used.
- I^O is recessive to I^A and I^B because it is not expressed in the heterozygote.
- I^A and I^B are **codominant**. This occurs when the heterozygous individual shows the effect of both alleles that they carry for the gene.

Worked example

A woman of blood group O has a baby with blood group B. Her partner has blood group AB.

(a) Use a Punnett square to explain how a baby can have a different blood group to both parents. **(3 marks)**

(b) State the probability that their next baby will also have group B. **(1 mark)**

The woman must have the genotype $I^O I^O$ and her partner must have the genotype $I^A I^B$.

The woman's gametes are all I^O but the man has two types of gamete: I^A and I^B.

	I^A	I^B
I^O	$I^A I^O$	$I^B I^O$
I^O	$I^A I^O$	$I^B I^O$

(b) = 50% or 1 in 2 or $\frac{1}{4}$

Worked example

In cattle, the allele C^R produces red hair and the allele C^W produces white hair. An animal with the genotype $C^R C^W$ has a mixture of red and white hairs, producing a colour called roan. Use a Punnett square to show the genotypes and phenotypes of the possible offspring that can be produced from a cross between two roan cattle. **(4 marks)**

		mother's genotype $C^R C^W$	
	gametes	C^R	C^W
father's genotype $C^R C^W$	C^R	$C^R C^R$ red	$C^R C^W$ roan
	C^W	$C^R C^W$ roan	$C^W C^W$ white

This means half their offspring are likely to have roan colour, a quarter will be white and a quarter will be red.

You might express this as 50% and 25%, or 1 in 4, for example.

Now try this

Describe how human ABO blood groups are inherited. **(3 marks)**

Variation and mutation

Causes of **variation** that influence phenotype include genetic variation and environmental variation. Genetic variation happens through **mutation**.

Causes of variation

Most phenotypic features in humans, e.g. hair colour, are caused by many genes. Each of these genes may have several

differences between individuals of the same kind

Most variations are caused by a combination of genes and environment.

caused by differences in alleles they have inherited, e.g. eye colour (**genetic variation**)

combination of both causes, e.g. weight, skin colour

caused by differences in conditions in which they developed, e.g. riding a bike, scars (**environmental variation**)

alleles, so the phenotype is the result of the **combination** of different alleles for different genes. This combination of alleles that an organism inherits is the result of sexual reproduction.

Mutation

A **mutation** or **genetic variant** is created if the sequence of bases in a gene is changed. A mutation in the gene's coding DNA can affect the phenotype of an organism. If the amino acid sequence is altered, the activity of the protein produced may also be altered. However:

- most genetic mutations have no effect on the phenotype

- some mutations have a small effect on the phenotype
- a single mutation can, rarely, significantly affect the phenotype.

A mutation may cause:
- a large change in the protein produced
- a small change in the protein
- no change at all in the protein produced.

The bigger the change to the protein, the larger the effect on how the body works.

Enzymes have a very specific shape that allows them to work effectively. Explain why a gene mutation can change the activity of an enzyme. Refer to the active site in your answer. **(3 marks)**

A gene mutation can change the base sequence in DNA. This may produce a different protein with a differently shaped active site. The shape of the active site controls how well an enzyme works. If the shape of the active site matches the shape of the substrate better, then the enzyme will work better. But if the shape of the active site is not as good a match, then the enzyme will not work so well.

---

1 Identical twins are genetically identical. Explain why they share many, but not all, of their characteristics. **(2 marks)**

2 Explain why a mutation in a body cell will not affect a person's phenotype. **(2 marks)**

Most mutations occur when DNA replicates before cell division. Most of them cause no change in the phenotype.

The Human Genome Project

The **Human Genome Project** is a collaboration between scientists to decode the **human genome** (the order of bases on all human chromosomes). The project was completed quickly because so many scientists worked on it at the same time. The work was published in 2003 and made freely available to scientists all over the world. The results are being used to develop new medicines and treatments for diseases.

Advantages and disadvantages of the Human Genome Project

Advantages

👍 Alerting people that they are at particular **risk** of certain diseases, e.g. types of cancer or heart disease. The person may be able to make lifestyle changes to reduce the chances of the disease developing.

👍 Distinguishing between different forms of diseases such as leukaemia or Alzheimer's disease, as some drugs are beneficial in some forms of these diseases but not in others.

👍 Allowing doctors to **tailor treatments** for some diseases to the individual, where specific alleles affect how a person will respond to treatment.

Disadvantages

👎 People who are at risk of certain diseases, e.g. cancer, may have to pay more to obtain life insurance.

👎 It may not be helpful to tell someone they are at risk of a condition for which there is currently no cure.

Worked example

Describe two possible developments as a result of decoding the human genome, and discuss the implications of these developments.   **(4 marks)**

One development is the identification of genes that can cause disease. Knowing if you have a faulty gene could help a person and their family prepare for its effects, but some people would prefer not to know if they have a faulty gene because then they would worry about it.

Another development is gene therapy. This involves replacing faulty alleles in body cells with healthy ones. This would allow the affected person to live a normal life. However, people will have to decide whether the faulty alleles are replaced in gametes, so that the healthy alleles could be passed on to children.

There are many possible answers for this question, because there are many new developments. Other possibilities include: creating personalised medicines, and identifying evolutionary relationships between humans and other organisms. As well as learning about new developments you need to be able to say what the implications are.

Now try this

1 Explain **one** way in which the Human Genome Project could be useful to doctors and their patients.

   (1 mark)

2 The genome of two different humans is not exactly the same. Explain why.   **(2 marks)**

Humans all share the same genes, but think carefully about alleles and base sequences.

Extended response – Genetics

There will be one or more 6-mark questions on your exam paper. For these questions, you will need to think scientifically and structure your answer logically, showing how the points you make are related to each other. You can revise the topics for this question, which is about **monohybrid inheritance**, on page 30.

Worked example

The ability to taste PTC is controlled by a dominant allele. A man and a woman who can both taste PTC have a daughter who can taste PTC but also a son who is unable to taste PTC. Explain these observations. **(6 marks)**

I will use T for the dominant taster allele, and t for the recessive allele.

The son cannot taste PTC, so he must be homozygous for the recessive allele, tt. This means he must have inherited a t allele from each of his parents. The genotype of both his parents must be Tt because they can taste PTC.

The Punnett square shows how he inherited this genotype.

		father's gametes	
		T	t
mother's gametes	T	TT taster	Tt taster
	t	Tt taster	tt non-taster

The Punnett square shows that the parents have a 25% (1 in 4) chance of having a child who cannot taste PTC. They have a 75% (3 in 4) chance of having a child who can taste PTC. Their daughter will have the genotype TT or Tt because she can taste PTC.

 PTC is phenylthiocarbamide. It is a substance that is tasteless to some people, but tastes bitter to others.

 Suggest suitable symbols for each allele, if none are given in the question.

 This part of the answer states and explains the possible genotypes of the son and his parents.

 Even in a long-answer question, a Punnett square or genetic diagram is a good way to display genetic information clearly.

 Remember to explain the possible outcomes in terms of probability, ratio or percentage.

The answer includes logical reasoning in the explanation. The phenotype corresponding to each possible genotype is shown in the Punnett square, giving further explanation for the observations.

Now try this

In guinea pigs, rough coat is dominant over smooth coat. Two rough-coated guinea pigs were bred together. They produced seven rough-coated offspring and two smooth-coated offspring. Use a genetic diagram to explain how this occurred. **(6 marks)**

Use R for the dominant allele and r for the recessive allele.

Evolution

Alfred Russel **Wallace** and Charles **Darwin** separately developed theories of evolution by means of natural selection, based on their own work and that of previous scientists. They presented their theory jointly in 1858, and it is still important in modern biology.

Natural selection

Individuals of a species show variation. This can mean that some individuals will be better able to survive in their environment and produce more healthy offspring than others. This is **natural selection**, where the environment (including climate and other organisms) selects which individuals pass on their **alleles** to the next generation.

Theory of evolution in modern biology

The theory of evolution is very important in modern biology:

- ☑ It helps us understand the relationships between different species of organisms.
- ☑ It explains how new species evolve.
- ☑ It explains how different species adapt to changes in their environment.

Darwin's theory

Adults usually produce more young than the environment can support when they are adults (overproduction). This produces a 'struggle for existence' by the young.	Some individuals have inherited **advantageous variations** in characteristics that are better adapted to the environment. These individuals will have a better chance of **survival** to adulthood.	Individuals with advantageous variations will pass their genes on to their young. The young may inherit the advantageous variations.	More individuals will have these advantageous variations in the next generation.
	Individuals with variations that are not as well adapted to the environment will be less likely to survive.	These individuals will not produce young.	

Worked example

African elephants are hunted illegally by poachers for their tusks. Elephants may be born tuskless due to a mutation. In 1930 in Uganda, only 1% of elephants were born without tusks. In 2010, 15% of females and 9% of male elephants were born without tusks. Explain this change using the theory of evolution. **(3 marks)**

Elephants with tusks are more likely to be poached and killed, so do not survive to pass on their alleles. Tuskless elephants are more likely to survive to pass on the allele for no tusks, so the allele for no tusks increases in frequency in the population.

One example of Darwin's theory is the development of antibiotic resistance in bacteria.

Doctors tell you to complete the full course of antibiotics, even if you feel better before the course is finished. If you do not finish taking a complete course of antibiotics, the bacteria resistant to the antibiotic can reproduce. This can result in an infection of antibiotic-resistant bacteria that is much harder to treat.

This is an example of where you may be asked to apply your understanding to a specific example that you may not be familiar with.

Now try this

Remember to use scientific terms like mutation and alleles, as well as explaining the effects on survival and passing on alleles.

Describe how Darwin's theory of evolution can explain antibiotic resistance in bacteria. **(4 marks)**

Human evolution

Some of the evidence we have for evolution leading to modern humans (*Homo sapiens*) comes from **fossils**. These include fossils of bones and teeth.

Species	Ardi (*Ardipithecus ramidus*)	Lucy (*Australopithecus afarensis*)	*Homo habilis* ('handy man')	*Homo erectus* ('upright man')	*Homo sapiens* ('wise'/modern man)
height	120 cm	107 cm	< 130 cm	179 cm	wide variety but generally taller than other species
when existed	4.4 million years ago	3.2 million years ago	2.4–1.4 million years ago	1.8–0.5 million years ago	since c. 200 000 years ago
brain size	350 cm³	400 cm³	500–600 cm³	850–1100 cm³	approx. 1200 cm³
other details	tree climber, also walked upright	walked upright, face ape-like	flat face like modern humans, used simple stone tools	long-distance walker, strongly built	user of complex tools

You do not need to remember details such as brain sizes but you do need to remember the names and the general trends.

Homo habilis and *Homo erectus* fossils were found by the archaeologists **Leakey** and his family. They wrote the first description of these early humans.

Stone tools

Stone tools also give us evidence of human evolution. The earliest stone tools are around 2.4 million years old. Over time more complex tools were made, and a greater range of tool types.

c. 2 million years old. A large stone that has had some chips flaked off it, e.g. simple hand axes

c. 40 000 years old. Made from fine flakes split from larger stones; many types of tool made this way, e.g. arrow head, spear head, scraper, knife

Explain how stone tools can be dated from their environment. **(3 marks)**

The amount of radiation in samples of sediment just above and below the layer in which the tools are found can be used to date the sediment and so give a range of dates when the tools were left there.

The stone used to make the tools is much older than the tools, so cannot be used to date when the tool was made.

1 Describe two ways that human-like species have evolved over the past 4.4 million years which can be seen from fossils. **(2 marks)**

2 Give two ways in which later stone tools were more complex than the earliest stone tools dating from about 2.4 million years ago. **(2 marks)**

Classification

Scientists used to classify living organisms into the following five big groups, called **kingdoms**. The kingdoms were Plants, Animals, Fungi, Protists and Prokaryotes. Scientists have now classified organisms into three **domains**.

Five-kingdom system

Carl Linnaeus originally proposed the classification of organisms into just two kingdoms, but this was later developed into five kingdoms. These are:
1 Plants
2 Animals
3 Fungi
4 Protists
5 Prokaryotes.

Three-domain system

Genetic research shows that the organisms which were grouped as prokaryotes in the kingdom system should be separated into two groups, which have been named **Eubacteria** and **Archaea**. This is because the genes of organisms in Archaea work more like those in the eukaryotes, while the genes of organisms in Eubacteria work a little differently.

This grouping forms the **three-domain** system of classification.

Eubacteria

Eukaryota
includes **Plants**
Animals
Fungi
Protoctista

prokaryotes

Archaea
mainly bacteria
that live in very
warm or salty
conditions

Worked example

The diagram shows the bones of the forelimbs of two living vertebrates. Explain how these pentadactyl limbs are evidence for evolution.

(4 marks)

humerus
radius
ulna
carpals
phalanges

human arm – for
holding and working
with objects

whale flipper –
for swimming
underwater

The limbs show the same basic pentadactyl structure. They have long bones supporting carpal bones and phalanges. This suggests that the human and the whale evolved from a shared ancestor. The differences between the limbs can be explained by evolution. The limbs have developed in different ways because they have adapted to different uses.

Many living vertebrates have the same **pentadactyl** (five-fingered) limb structure.

Notice that this answer explains ways in which DNA differs between different groups of organisms, and points out that closely-related organisms have more similarities in their DNA.

Worked example

Suggest how studying DNA can help scientists to work out the evolutionary relationships between different groups of organisms. **(3 marks)**

Scientists can examine the structure of the DNA in the cells, e.g. whether it is formed into linear chromosomes or is circular. They can also find out how much non-coding DNA it contains. Then they can find the base sequence in the DNA of different organisms. The more closely related the organisms are, the more similarities there will be in their DNA base sequences.

Now try this

1 Describe the three-domain system of classification.
(3 marks)

2 Give two ways in which genetic analysis has led to the five-kingdom system being replaced by the three-domain system. **(2 marks)**

Selective breeding

Selective breeding is when plants or animals with certain desirable characteristics are chosen to breed together, so that offspring will be produced that **inherit** these characteristics. This produces **new breeds** of animals and **new varieties** of plants. Selective breeding has taken place over thousands of years, but more recently **genetic engineering** has been developed as a way of manipulating genetics. You can learn about this on page 41.

Selective breeding in plants

| Plants with good features are crossed, e.g. plants that have good yield, are drought tolerant, or need less fertiliser. | → | Plants grown from seeds of these crosses are selected for their good features and crossed with each other. | → | Selection and crossing is repeated many times until a high-yielding variety is produced. |

Reasons for selective breeding

Plants and animals are selectively bred for:

- ☑ disease resistance
- ☑ increased yield
- ☑ better ability to cope with difficult conditions
- ☑ faster growth
- ☑ better flavour.

Worked example

Describe how a farmer would breed cattle that have a large milk yield. **(4 marks)**

The farmer would choose a cow that produced lots of milk and cross her with a bull whose mother produced a lot of milk. The farmer would then choose the female offspring who produce lots of milk and cross them with a male whose mother had a high milk yield. The farmer would do this for many generations.

Worked example

The graph shows the average milk yield per cow from 1957 to 2007. The increase is mainly the result of selective breeding. Over the same period there has been an increase in cows suffering from mastitis (an inflammation of the udders), problems with their legs and reduced fertility. A farming newspaper reported this in an article entitled 'Selective breeding has improved dairy farming'. Evaluate this statement. **(4 marks)**

The graph shows that the milk yield per cow has more than doubled over these 50 years so this is useful for the farmer.

Advantage

However, the cows are having more problems with their legs and udders which may be because they are producing so much milk, so this is an animal welfare issue.

Ethical issue

It also costs the farmer more in veterinary bills.

Practical issue

I think that selective breeding to produce a high-yielding breed of cows is a good thing, but this should not be done at the expense of animal welfare.

Now try this

1 Give one advantage and one disadvantage of selective breeding. **(2 marks)**

2 Describe how a farmer could breed sheep that have thick wool. **(3 marks)**

3 Describe one problem of selective breeding in crop plants. **(2 marks)**

You can draw your own conclusion as long as it clearly relates to the information given and the benefits and risks identified.

Genetic engineering

Genetic engineering is changing the **genome** (the DNA) of an organism, often by introducing genes from another to create **genetically modified organisms** (GMOs).

How genetic engineering works

Genes can be transferred from any kind of organism to any other kind of organism, e.g. bacteria, humans, other animals, plants.

The gene for a characteristic is 'cut out' of a chromosome using enzymes.

The gene is inserted into a chromosome inside the nucleus of a cell in a different organism.

The cell of this organism now produces the characteristic from the gene.

Worked example

Human insulin is a hormone used by many patients with diabetes. Bacteria have been genetically modified to carry the human insulin gene. The bacteria are then grown in large quantities to produce the human insulin.
Explain why bacteria had to be modified to make human insulin and describe how the GM bacteria were produced. **(3 marks)**

Bacteria don't normally produce human insulin, so they had to be modified to make it. The gene for making insulin was cut out of a human chromosome. The gene was then inserted into the bacterial chromosome, so that the bacterium made the insulin.

GM crops

GM crop plants have been genetically modified to give them new characteristics, such as:

- resistance to attack by insects
- resistance to **herbicides**, so that fields can be sprayed to kill weeds, but not the crop.

These characteristics can help the crop grow better and produce more food (an increased **yield**).

It is possible to give an advantage and then a disadvantage in the same sentence. Or you can give an advantage in one sentence and then a disadvantage in the next sentence.

Worked example

A sheep has been genetically modified to produce a protein in its milk that can be used to treat serious lung diseases in humans. Explain the advantages and disadvantages of this. **(4 marks)**

The protein is secreted in milk so the sheep is not harmed to produce the protein, although some people think it is unethical to use animals for the benefit of humans. The protein treats serious lung disease so is very beneficial to human health. However, in developing the genetically modified sheep a lot of embryos would have been made that did not successfully express the gene, so a lot of embryos are wasted to produce a GM sheep.

Now try this

1 Define **genetic engineering**. **(2 marks)**

2 Scientists have produced GM crop plants that are resistant to herbicides. The field can be sprayed with herbicide that kills weeds but not the crop.
Give **one** possible advantage of this and **one** possible disadvantage. **(2 marks)**

41

Tissue culture

Plant and animal tissue can be used to produce **cell cultures**. This means you can make many identical copies of a special organism, for example, one that has been genetically modified. It also means that drugs can be tested on cell cultures instead of animals.

Plant tissue culture

tissue sample cut from parent plant

agar jelly containing plant hormones and nutrients

samples grow into tiny plants

trays of compost

> This process is similar for other kinds of cells.

Advantages of using cell cultures

Uses of animal cell cultures	Uses of plant cell cultures
test the effect of drugs and other chemicals on cells	produce hundreds or thousands of identical plants (clones) from just one parent plant, e.g. genetically modified plants
check for cancer cells in a sample from a patient	cells can be grown in culture to make plant products, e.g. paclitaxel used to treat cancer
produce important proteins, e.g. antibodies	produce disease-free plants

Worked example

Suggest an advantage of testing drugs on animal cell cultures rather than on animals. **(2 marks)**

Testing drugs on animals means using a lot of animals and it may cause them harm. It also takes up a lot of space to test drugs on animals and cell cultures use very little space. You can test drugs on large numbers of cells in cell cultures and there are no ethical issues if the drug damages the cells.

> There are several advantages but you can get full marks for just one advantage as long as you explain why it is an advantage.

Worked example

Scientists have made a genetically modified cotton plant which contains a protein that kills insect pests. The scientists want to make many copies of this plant so they can test the plant grows well. Explain the advantage of tissue culture in this process. **(3 marks)**

Thousands of identical plants can be made from just one parent plant. They can be grown quickly in a small space. As they are genetically identical to the parent plant they are very useful for testing.

> Remember you need to make 3 points to gain 3 marks.

Now try this

1 Explain why the plantlets produced by plant tissue culture are genetically identical. **(2 marks)**
2 Describe how tissue culture can be used to make many identical cauliflower plants. **(2 marks)**

> This question checks that you really understand what is going on in plant tissue culture.

Insect-resistant plants

An example of genetic engineering in crop plants is the introduction of genes that give **insect resistance**.

Creating Bt plants

| The bacterium **Bacillus thuringiensis** naturally produces a chemical that is poisonous to insect pests such as caterpillars. This chemical is called **Bt toxin**. | → | The gene for Bt toxin can be cut out of the bacterial DNA and inserted into the DNA of a plant cell using Agrobacterium tumefaciens. | → | Plants grown from these cells produce the Bt toxin. When an insect tries to eat them, the poison kills the insect pest. |

Agrobacterium tumefaciens naturally infects plant cells, and so is a useful vector for making transgenic plants.

Using Bt plants

There are advantages and disadvantages of introducing genes for insect resistance into crop plants.

Advantages	Disadvantages
👍 Crop damage is reduced so crop yield should increase. 👍 Less chemical insecticide is needed so other harmless and useful insects are less likely to be harmed (better for biodiversity).	👎 Seed from transgenic plants is more expensive than seed from non-transgenic varieties. 👎 Insect pests may become resistant to Bt toxin. 👎 Bt gene may transfer to closely related wild plants by pollination, which would make those plants resistant to pests too.

Worked example

Explain how genetic modification with the Bt toxin gene could increase food production. **(2 marks)**

Damage to a plant's leaves by an insect pest will reduce the amount of food that a plant makes by photosynthesis. This will reduce the rate of plant growth, including growth of the parts of the plant that we eat. Bt toxin kills insect pests that eat the leaves, so crop yield should increase.

You need to explain how insects reduce crop yields as well as understanding that the Bt toxin gene kills insects.

Now try this

1 State why insect-resistant crop plants are less likely to be grown in poorer countries. **(1 mark)**

Think about the costs of GM seed.

2 Describe how a wheat plant could be genetically modified to produce Bt toxin. **(4 marks)**

Meeting population needs

A growing human **population** needs more food. Agricultural solutions to this include using **fertilisers** and **biological control**.

Advantages and disadvantages of fertilisers

👍 Fertilisers contain nutrients, including nitrogen, phosphorus and potassium, that help crops to grow well.

👍 They increase crop yields providing more food for people.

👍 It is a good way to use animal waste (manure) from farms.

👎 Excess fertiliser can pollute waterways, causing **eutrophication**.

👎 Artificial fertilisers are expensive to make.

👎 Artificial fertilisers can reduce soil biodiversity.

See page 99 for more information on eutrophication.

Advantages and disadvantages of biological control

Biological control uses a natural predator, parasite or disease of the pest to keep the pest population low.

👍 The pest cannot become resistant.

👍 If well chosen, the control agent is **specific** to the pest.

👍 It avoids using chemical pesticides which can leave harmful residues and kill useful organisms.

👎 Biological control does not get rid of the pest completely.

👎 The control agent may become a pest itself.

Worked example

Red spider mite is a pest of greenhouse crops. A predatory mite that feeds on the pest can be used as a biological control. Explain the advantages and disadvantages of this. **(3 marks)**

The predatory mite feeds on the red spider mite so it gets rid of the pest but not other useful insects. The red spider mite cannot develop resistance to it, and the predatory mite only needs to be introduced once because it reproduces in the greenhouse. A disadvantage is that it does not get rid of the red spider mite completely. When the red spider mite population falls, the predatory mite runs out of food so its population falls as well.

> You need to apply your understanding of biological control to specific examples like this.

Now try this

1 Give **one** advantage and **one** disadvantage of using artificial fertilisers. **(2 marks)**

2 Explain why biological control does not completely remove a pest. **(2 marks)**

Extended response – Genetic modification

There will be one or more 6-mark questions on your exam paper. For these questions, you will need to think scientifically, and structure your answer logically, showing how the points you make are related to each other. You can revise the topics for this question, which is about the **advantages and disadvantages of genetic modification of crops**, on pages 41 to 43.

Worked example

Some crop plants have been modified to produce a toxin when their cells are damaged. This toxin kills caterpillars when they eat it. Evaluate the factors that should be considered before deciding to grow these crops on a large scale. **(6 marks)**

First you would need to consider whether this method of killing caterpillars is effective in increasing crop yield. Genetically modifying the crop will be expensive, so tests will need to be carried out to find out whether the increased yield brings in enough income to offset the cost of buying genetically modified seeds to plant.

You would also need to know whether the toxin is harmful to people eating the crop. Tests must be carried out to make sure the crop is safe to eat. It is also important that customers are happy to buy this crop. Some people do not like the idea of eating genetically modified food, and choose not to buy it.

Growing this crop might save time and costs for the farmer, because it has a toxin in the crop so the farmer does not need to buy a pesticide to kill the caterpillars. The toxin is always there so caterpillars should be killed as soon as they start to eat the crop. Also, there will not be any harmful pesticide residues left on the crop. If the farmer sprays his crops with a pesticide instead, this could harm useful insects as well as the caterpillars.

There is a possible ethical issue if the toxin gene transferred somehow to wild plants. This could possibly lead to wild plants containing a toxin, which could kill insects and cause problems in food chains. On balance I think it would be a good idea to grow this crop, but only after the necessary tests have been carried out.

Do not be put off if you have not met this specific example before. You are given all the information you need. Think about identifying advantages and disadvantages, and drawing a conclusion.

Consider what the alternative to using the GM crop might be, as this will help you to weigh up the different factors that have to be considered.

Other answers

The answer to this question could have covered other issues, such as how the development of resistance to Bt toxin by insects will affect the benefits of using GM crops. It could also have covered the problem that many people will not buy food from GM crops as they do not trust that it is safe. What matters in this answer is that it covers all that the question asks, and is presented in a clear and logical order.

Now try this

Some children do not produce enough growth hormone, which leads to a slow growth rate in childhood. Scientists can genetically modify bacteria to produce human growth hormone. Explain how they could do this. **(6 marks)**

Health and disease

The World Health Organization defines **health** as 'a state of complete physical, mental and social well-being'. There are many different **diseases** with different causes.

What is health?

health

such as how you feel about yourself → mental well-being

such as eating and sleeping well, and being free from disease → physical well-being

social well-being ← such as how well you get on with other people

Types of disease

Diseases may be **communicable** (they can be passed from one person to another) or **non-communicable** (not passed between people). A **pathogen** is an organism that causes an infectious disease.

Communicable	Non-communicable
rapid variation in number of cases over time	number of cases changes only gradually
cases are often localised	cases may be more widely spread
e.g. malaria, typhoid, cholera	e.g. cancer, diabetes, heart disease

Worked example

Chalara fungus sometimes kills ash trees directly, but sometimes it makes the tree more likely to be infected by other pathogens which kill the tree. Suggest how this happens. **(2 marks)**

The fungus damages the bark and the cells of the ash tree, making it easier for other pathogens to infect the tree.

HIV is a pathogen that makes it easier for other pathogens to infect a person. In the case of HIV, this happens because of damage to the immune system.

Pathogens

Pathogens include bacteria and viruses, fungi and protists. When a few pathogens **infect** you (get inside your body) they can reproduce very rapidly. Large numbers of pathogens make you ill.

Bacteria are much smaller than human cells.

Viruses are much smaller than bacteria.

bacterium
Bacteria may release **toxins** (poisons) that make us feel ill. Some types of bacteria invade and destroy body cells.

virus
Viruses take over a body cell's DNA, causing the cell to make **toxins** or causing damage when new viruses are released from cells.

fungi
Fungi are eukaryotic organisms.

protist
Protists are eukaryotic organisms. Many are free-living but some are pathogens.

Pathogens make you feel ill when they damage cells or change how they work.

Now try this

1 Name four types of organism that can act as a pathogen. **(4 marks)**

2 A stroke is caused when a blood clot blocks an artery in the brain. This stops oxygen reaching part of the brain and nerve cells die. State whether a stroke is a communicable or non-communicable disease. Give a reason for your answer. **(2 marks)**

Common infections

Different kinds of pathogens can cause different diseases with different symptoms. You need to be able to describe the **infections** given on this page.

Infection	Type of pathogen	Main symptoms
cholera	bacterium	• watery, pale-coloured **diarrhoea**, often in large amounts (watery faeces)
malaria	protist	• **fever** (high temperature) • **weakness** • chills • sweating
HIV/AIDS	virus	• mild flu-like symptoms may occur when first infected • often, no symptoms for a long time • eventually, **repeated infections** (e.g. TB) that would not be a problem if immune system was working properly
tuberculosis (TB)	bacterium	• lung damage seen in **blood speckled mucus** • **weight loss** • **fever** and chills • night sweats
Ebola	virus	• internal bleeding and fever (**haemorrhagic fever**) • severe headache • muscle pain • vomiting • diarrhoea (frequent watery faeces)
stomach ulcers	bacterium	• **inflammation** in stomach causing pain • bleeding in stomach
ash die-back *Chalara*	fungus	• leaf loss • bark **lesions** (damage) • **dieback** of top of tree (crown)

Worked example

Describe a communicable disease caused by a bacterium and the symptoms of the disease.

(3 marks)

TB is a communicable disease. Two of its symptoms are blood speckled mucus and weight loss.

You could choose any of the other communicable diseases in the table. One mark is for naming the disease, then two marks for two symptoms.

Now try this

Give one example of a pathogen from each of the following groups, describing two signs of the infection it causes:

Make sure you know which group each pathogen belongs to.

(a) virus   **(2 marks)**
(b) protist   **(2 marks)**
(c) fungus   **(2 marks)**

How pathogens spread

Understanding how pathogens are spread can help us to find ways of **reducing** or **preventing** their spread.

Malaria

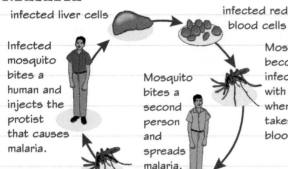

infected liver cells

infected red blood cells

Infected mosquito bites a human and injects the protist that causes malaria.

Mosquito bites a second person and spreads malaria.

Mosquito becomes infected with parasite when it takes a blood meal.

The protist that causes malaria is spread by a **vector**, the mosquito.

Watch out! Vectors are not pathogens. Vectors carry pathogens from one person to another. Vectors are one way infectious diseases are spread.

HIV

The human immunodeficiency virus, **HIV**, enters the blood and reproduces inside white blood cells, causing white blood cell destruction.

Eventually so many white blood cells are destroyed that the immune system cannot work properly. This stage is called **AIDS**. The person becomes ill with a disease, such as tuberculosis, that would not be a problem if their immune system was working properly.

Ebola virus

The **Ebola virus** causes **haemorrhagic fever**. The virus infects humans from other infected people, infected animals or objects that have been in contact with the virus. The virus infects:

• liver cells
• cells from the lining of the blood vessels
• white blood cells.

It multiplies inside these cells and destroys them. This causes fever, severe headache, muscle pain, extreme weakness, vomiting, diarrhoea, and internal and external bleeding.

Reducing the spread of pathogens

Disease (cause)	Ways to reduce or prevent its spread
cholera (bacteria)	• boil water to kill bacteria before drinking • wash hands thoroughly after using toilet to prevent spread by touch
tuberculosis (bacteria)	• ventilate buildings adequately to reduce chance of breathing in bacteria in droplets of mucus coughed out by an infected person • diagnose infected people promptly and give antibiotics to kill tuberculosis bacteria • isolate infected people so they cannot pass the infection to others
malaria (protists)	• prevent mosquito vectors biting people, by killing mosquitoes or keeping them off skin (e.g. by using a mosquito net)
stomach ulcers (bacteria)	• cook food thoroughly to kill bacteria • wash hands thoroughly before preparing food to avoid transfer
Haemorrhagic fever (Ebola virus)	• keep infected people isolated because the virus is easily spread • wear fully protective clothing while working with infected people or dead bodies

Now try this

Using malaria as an example, explain the difference between a **pathogen** and a **vector**. **(2 marks)**

STIs

Chlamydia and HIV are sexually transmitted infections (**STIs**) spread by sexual activity. *Chlamydia* is a bacterium, and HIV is a virus.

Virus lifecycle

Viruses infect host cells. They multiply by the **lytic** cycle or the **lysogenic** cycle.

1 Virus attaches to host cell.

2 Virus enters cell and injects its DNA or RNA into the cell.

Lytic Cycle

Lysogenic Cycle

4 The DNA or RNA and virus proteins are packaged together to make new viruses. These are released from the cell, which usually destroys the host cell.

3 Virus RNA or DNA copies itself and causes new virus proteins to be made, using the organelles in the host cell.

> The virus is actually much smaller than this compared to the host cell.

In the lysogenic cycle, the virus inserts its DNA into the chromosomes of the host cell. It is called a **provirus**. The provirus replicates with the rest of the host DNA every time the host cell divides. The provirus can stay dormant for a long time like this. At some stage, the provirus can become active and make new viruses in the lytic cycle.

Spread of STIs

Chlamydia bacteria can be spread by contact with sexual fluid from an infected partner. An infected mother can pass *Chlamydia* to her baby during birth.

Common methods of **HIV transmission** are:
- unprotected sex with an infected partner
- sharing needles with an infected person
- transmission from infected mother to foetus
- infection from blood products.

Reducing or preventing STIs

The spread of many STIs can be reduced or prevented by:
- using **condoms** during sexual intercourse
- **screening people**, including pregnant women
- **screening blood** transfusions
- supplying intravenous drug abusers with **sterile needles** (HIV)
- treating infected people using **antibiotics** (for *Chlamydia* and other bacterial infections).

Worked example

A newborn baby's eyes are infected with *Chlamydia*. Explain how this could happen. **(1 mark)**

During birth, the baby's eyes and lungs may become contaminated with vaginal fluid containing the bacteria.

> Pathogens enter the body through natural openings, so the baby's eyes, nose and mouth are places where pathogens can enter the body easily.

Now try this

1 State what STIs are and how they are spread. **(2 marks)**
2 During sexual intercourse a man places a condom over his penis. Explain how this reduces his risk of being infected with an STI. **(1 mark)**

Human defences

The human body has both physical barriers and chemical defences to give protection against pathogens. **Physical barriers** make it hard for pathogens to enter the body. **Chemical defences** are chemicals that are produced to kill or make pathogens inactive.

Chemical and physical defences

Chemical defences
Lysozyme enzyme in tears kills bacteria by digesting their cell walls.

Lysozyme enzyme is also present in saliva and mucus.

Hydrochloric acid in stomach kills pathogens in food and drink.

Physical barriers
Unbroken **skin** forms a protective barrier because it is too thick for most pathogens to get through.

Sticky **mucus** in the breathing passages and lungs traps pathogens. **Cilia** on the cells lining the lungs move in a wave-like motion, moving mucus and trapped pathogens out of lungs towards the back of the throat where it is swallowed.

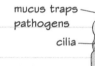
mucus traps pathogens
cilia move mucus away from lungs
cilia
epithelial cells

Remember that epithelial cells line the surface of tubes.

Worked example

Cilia move mucus away from the lungs. Describe how this protects the body from pathogens. **(3 marks)**

It stops pathogens entering the lungs where they can cause disease. When the mucus gets to the throat it is swallowed and the pathogens are destroyed by the acid in the stomach.

Cilia are tiny hairs on the surfaces of cells that move together in a rhythm to move substances along, such as mucus. Their movement is a bit like a crowd of people doing a Mexican wave.

Worked example

Chemicals in cigarette smoke paralyse the cilia in the epithelium of the airways. Smokers are more likely than non-smokers to suffer from lung infections. Explain why. **(2 marks)**

When the cilia are paralysed, they cannot move the mucus containing pathogens back up to the throat. The mucus travels down into the lungs, carrying pathogens with them.

Now try this

1 Give **one** example of a physical barrier and **one** example of a chemical defence that prevents pathogens entering the body. **(2 marks)**

2 Explain why someone with a skin burn can develop an infection. **(2 marks)**

The immune system

The **immune system** helps to protect the body by attacking pathogens if they manage to enter the body. **Lymphocytes** are part of this immune system.

1 Each pathogen has unique **antigens** on its surface.

These lymphocytes are not activated.

2 A **lymphocyte** with an **antibody** that fits the antigen is activated.

3 The lymphocyte **divides** many times to produce clones of identical lymphocytes.

4 Some of the lymphocytes produce lots of antibodies which stick to the pathogen and destroy it. Other lymphocytes stay in the blood as **memory lymphocytes**, ready to respond immediately if the same antigen returns.

Antibodies

The antibodies produced by a white blood cell are **specific** for one particular kind of pathogen. This means they can only destroy that kind of pathogen. They cannot destroy another kind of bacterium or virus.

Immunity

White blood cells respond to infection by making antibodies.

Amount of antibody in bloodstream in arbitrary units

first infection

second infection

immunity level

Time in weeks

The memory lymphocytes are made after the infection and then respond more quickly to another infection by the pathogen.

This is called the **secondary response**.

Worked example

Explain why there is a delay of a few days between a person becoming infected by a pathogen for the first time and antibodies being made. **(2 marks)**

It takes time for lymphocytes to identify the antigens on the pathogen, and to secrete specific antibodies.

The secondary response is much faster because memory cells are already present, and can secrete specific antibodies immediately.

Worked example

Pathogens have antigens that are foreign to the body. When a pathogen enters the body, the body is exposed to these antigens. Describe two responses triggered by the antigens. **(2 marks)**

The antigens trigger an immune response which causes the production of antibodies.
They also trigger the production of memory lymphocytes.

Now try this

Describe how the immune system of the human body defends against disease. **(3 marks)**

Immunisation

Immunisation is when you give a person a vaccine to prevent them becoming ill from a disease.

How vaccines work

| A **vaccine** contains antigens from the pathogen, often in the form of dead or weakened pathogens. | → | The person's lymphocytes produce antibodies against the pathogen and also memory lymphocytes. | → | If the person becomes infected with the real pathogen, the memory lymphocytes will give a very rapid secondary response to the pathogen. This means the person is very unlikely to become ill. |

This form of the pathogen is **inactive** and cannot cause the disease in the person receiving the vaccine.

Advantages and disadvantages of immunisation

👍 Immunity is produced without being ill.

👍 Immunity lasts a long time, often for life.

👍 If most people are immune, then the few people who are unvaccinated are also less likely to catch the disease. This is called **herd immunity**.

👎 Some people get a mild reaction of swelling or soreness, or a mild form of the disease.

👎 Very rarely, a person has a major harmful reaction.

Worked example

Describe how a vaccine can protect you for life. **(2 marks)**

Once you have received the vaccine, the immune system makes antibodies but also memory lymphocytes which stay in the body for a long time. If you ever catch the disease 'for real', these memory cells divide very quickly and produce huge numbers of antibodies.

Make sure you refer to memory lymphocytes being formed as a result of vaccination.

Worked example

Explain why immunisation only protects you against one particular disease. **(2 marks)**

Each pathogen has a particular antigen. The immune system produces antibodies that are exactly the right shape to fit on to these antigens. Other pathogens have antigens of a different shape, so one kind of antibody cannot bind to a different kind of antigen.

You sometimes hear people say that a vaccine is a 'small dose of the disease'. This is wrong. The vaccine contains antigens from the pathogen and is not necessarily a small amount. However it is in a safe form, e.g. the pathogen is dead or weakened. And you are not given the disease, just antigens from the pathogen that causes the disease.

Now try this

 1 Describe the difference between a vaccine and immunisation. **(2 marks)**

 Immunisation and vaccination mean the same thing.

 2 Sometimes a person needs to receive a second (booster) vaccination. Explain the advantage of this. **(2 marks)**

You need to use your understanding to think why it might be helpful for a person to have a second vaccination of the same antigens a short time after the first vaccination.

Treating infections

Antibiotics can be used to treat bacterial infections.

Antibiotics

Antibiotics are medicines that **kill bacteria** inside the body. Specific bacteria are only killed by a specific antibiotic, so the correct antibiotic must be used. Deaths from bacterial diseases have greatly decreased where antibiotics are used. **Penicillin** is an example of an antibiotic.

> Some bacteria are becoming **resistant** to some antibiotics. This means that the antibiotic is no longer effective at killing or inhibiting them.

Worked example

Describe how antibiotics kill bacteria.   **(2 marks)**

Antibiotics inhibit cell processes in the bacterium but not the host organism. For example, some antibiotics stop bacterial cell walls forming properly. This does not harm the host animal because animal cells do not have cell walls.

> Do not confuse **antibiotics** and **antibodies**. They are very different things!

Effect of antibiotics on bacteria

The effect of antiseptics, antibiotics or plant extracts on the growth of bacteria can be studied on a **bacterial culture** in a **Petri dish**.

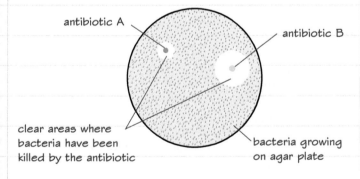

antibiotic A

antibiotic B

clear areas where bacteria have been killed by the antibiotic

bacteria growing on agar plate

Maths skills — Comparing the effects of antibiotics

You can **calculate** the cross-sectional area of the clear zone using the formula πr^2 (where r = the radius of the circle of the clear zone). This allows you to **compare** how effective different antibiotics are. So if, in the example on the left, $r = 8\,mm$ for antibiotic A and $14\,mm$ for antibiotic B, then:

Area for antibiotic A = $\pi \times 8^2 = 201\,mm^2$

Area for antibiotic B = $\pi \times 14^2 = 615\,mm^2$

Antibiotic B is the more effective antibiotic for this bacterial culture.

Now try this

1 Explain why doctors do not prescribe antibiotics if a patient has the flu virus.   **(1 mark)**

2 One antibiotic works by stopping protein synthesis in bacteria but not in human cells. Explain why this antibiotic kills bacteria but is safe to use in humans.   **(2 marks)**

Aseptic techniques

When working with microorganisms, you need to use **aseptic techniques**. These help to prevent other microorganisms from the air and surfaces from contaminating cultures when they are being prepared. Several techniques can help prevent this.

① Sterilising dishes and culture media

Sterilisation kills microorganisms.

* Petri dishes can be **sterilised** by autoclaving or heating to a high temperature.
* Culture media (the substances that the microorganisms grow on, such as nutrient agar) are sterilised by heating to a high temperature.

② Sterilising inoculating loops

The loop is sterilised in a hot flame and then cooled, before using it to transfer microorganisms to the growth medium.

The Petri dish is not completely sealed as this would encourage the growth of anaerobic bacteria which are likely to be pathogens.

③ Sealing Petri dishes

The lid is secured to the dish with adhesive tape to stop microorganisms from the air getting in. Vials containing bacteria must be kept covered for the same reason.

Worked example

Cultures of microorganisms should be incubated at a maximum temperature of 25 °C in school and college laboratories. Explain why. **(2 marks)**

Temperatures higher than this encourage rapid growth in bacteria. This includes pathogenic bacteria that are harmful to humans.

When microorganisms are grown in industry, they are cultured at higher temperatures than 25 °C because they are not handled by people. The microorganisms grow more quickly at these higher temperatures, but there is no risk that people will get infected by the bacteria.

Now try this

1 Give **three** ways in which cultures of microorganisms can easily be contaminated with other microorganisms during preparation. **(3 marks)**

2 Give **two** reasons why good aseptic technique is important. **(2 marks)**

Investigating microbial cultures

Practical skills   You can investigate the **effect of antiseptics, antibiotics or plant extracts on the growth of bacteria** by placing paper discs of the test substances on to a bacterial lawn (a Petri dish of nutrient agar covered in a layer of bacteria) and incubating them for a few days.

Core practical

Apparatus

- bacterial lawn plate
- paper discs soaked in test substances
- sterile forceps
- sticky tape
- marker pen
- Bunsen burner + heat-resistant mat

You might investigate how effective different concentrations of the same substance are at killing bacteria. Or you might investigate different kinds of antiseptic, antibiotic or plant extract. If comparing different substances, think about how to prepare the extracts so the test is fair.

Method

1 Turn the bacterial plate upside down and mark the base into sections – one section for each test disc. Label each section with the substance or concentration used.

2 Turn the plate the right way up. Lift the lid of the dish just enough to be able to place a disc on the lawn.

3 Use the sterile forceps to place one paper disc on to the bacterial lawn in the correct section. Then briefly flame the forceps in a blue Bunsen flame to sterilise them again.

4 Repeat step 3 for each disc.

5 Tape the lid to the base of the dish without completely sealing it, to avoid the risk of harmful anaerobic bacteria growing.

6 Incubate the plate for a few days at 25 °C.

Remember: aseptic techniques are needed to help prevent contamination. You can revise this topic on page 54.

Results

Accurately measure the diameter of any clear area in mm.

There are different ways to measure the diameters, e.g. squared paper, ruler. Choose a way that will give you the most precise values.

Conclusion

The larger the diameter of a clear area around a disc, the better the test substance was at killing bacteria.

Maths skills   Remember that you could also calculate the cross-sectional area of each clear area using πr^2, where r is the radius (half the diameter).

Now try this

The table shows the results of one investigation into the effect of some plant extracts on bacterial growth.

(a) Display these results on a chart. **(2 marks)**

(b) Draw a conclusion from the results. **(1 mark)**

Plant extract	Diameter of clear area (mm)	Cross sectional area of clear area/mm²
neem	15	177
oregano	17	227
lemongrass	5	20
thyme	10	79

New medicines

Medicines are chemicals that are used to treat the cause or signs of an illness. Scientists are continually developing new medicines. New medicines must be extensively tested before doctors can **prescribe** them to patients. There are several steps of testing.

Development and testing

 Discovery

New medicines are **discovered**, e.g. by screening organisms to see if they produce antibiotics that kill bacteria. They are then **developed** through a series of stages.

 Clinical trials: stage 1

healthy volunteer

very small **dose** of drug

To check that the drug is not **toxic** (harmful).

Medical drugs are prescribed (given) by doctors to help patients who are ill.

 Preclinical testing (in the lab)

cultures of cells   cultures of tissues

animals

Antibiotics are **tested** in the lab to make sure the medicine gets into cells without harming them, and damages pathogens inside cells.

 Clinical trials: stage 2

different doses of drug

patient with the disease that the new drug is developed for

To test **efficacy** (whether it works) and to find the **optimum** dose (the dose that works best).

Worked example

Explain why a new medicine is not tested on lots of people straight away. **(3 marks)**

This is to make sure there are no harmful side effects and also to make sure it works on people. It would be unethical to give the medicine to lots of people before it was tested for safety and to see if it works on people.

Now try this

There are several different possible answers here, but you only need to think of two of them.

1 Two antibiotics are effective in treating a bacterial infection. When tested on a Petri dish of bacteria, antibiotic A produces a larger clear zone than antibiotic B. Suggest **two** reasons that explain why a doctor chooses to prescribe antibiotic B to a patient. **(2 marks)**

2 Suggest **one** advantage and **one** disadvantage of using animals as models for testing new drugs rather than direct testing on humans. **(2 marks)**

Non-communicable diseases

Many non-communicable diseases are caused by the **interaction of several factors**. Having several factors can increase the risk of developing a disease.

Factors that affect the risk of developing non-communicable diseases

Genes (inherited factors): Different alleles of a gene may be more prone to mutation (e.g. in breast cancer) or how well you absorb nutrients (e.g. in diseases related to diet). These factors may be more common in particular ethnic groups.

Age: The older the body, the more likely that cells may develop mutations which lead to cancer.

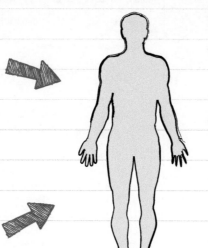

Sex: The female hormone oestrogen has protective effects that men do not get.

Environmental: Air pollution can cause lung diseases; poisons in food and drink can damage the body.

Lifestyle factors: The way we live, including diet, alcohol, smoking and exercise, can affect our risk of developing many diseases. You can find out more about lifestyle factors on pages 58 and 59.

Some non-communicable diseases caused by these factors include cancer, cardiovascular (heart) disease, lung and liver diseases, and dietary diseases. Rates of these diseases are different between different groups of people in a country, or in different countries, according to individual exposure to these risk factors.

Worked example

The graph shows the number of deaths from heart disease in the USA for one year.

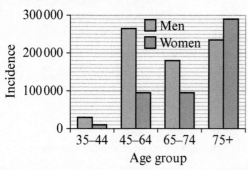

(a) Describe the effect of age on deaths from heart disease shown in the chart. **(2 marks)**

The death rate from heart disease is at least twice as high in men compared to women until the 75+ age group, when more women die from heart disease than men.

(b) Women produce the hormone oestrogen until the menopause (at about 50). Suggest whether the chart supports the idea that oestrogen can protect against heart disease. **(2 marks)**

The idea is not clearly supported, because the 65–74 category is about the same as the 45–64 group, but it does increase greatly in the 75+ group.

Now try this

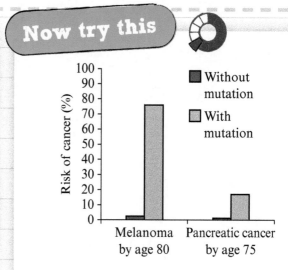

The chart shows the risk of developing some types of cancer. It compares people with a particular mutation in a specific gene with people without this mutation.

(a) Explain why the risk of cancer is shown as a percentage. **(2 marks)**

(b) Do these data support the hypothesis that this mutation increases a person's chance of developing cancer? Explain your answer. **(2 marks)**

Alcohol and smoking

Lifestyle factors including **drinking alcohol** and **smoking** increase the risk of non-communicable diseases by changing how the body works and increasing the levels of **toxins** (poisons) in your body.

Alcohol and disease

Ethanol (found in alcohol) is poisonous to cells. When absorbed from the gut, it passes first to the **liver** to be broken down. So liver cells are more likely than other cells to be damaged, leading to liver disease, e.g. cirrhosis.

> This can lead to low birth weight in babies whose mothers smoke.

The damage caused by smoking

Nicotine is addictive.

Carbon monoxide reduces how much oxygen the blood can carry.

Chemicals in **tar** are **carcinogens** that cause cancers, particularly of mouth and lungs.

Substances in cigarettes can cause blood vessels to narrow, increasing blood pressure. This can lead to **cardiovascular diseases** such as heart attack or strokes.

Worked example

The graph shows the incidence of liver disease and the mean ethanol consumption per person per year for different countries.

Describe and explain the relationship shown in the graph. **(2 marks)**.

As the amount of alcohol consumed increases, the incidence of liver disease also increases. This is because ethanol is poisonous, particularly to liver cells.

This is a scatter diagram. It is good for showing a link (**correlation**) between two factors. This graph shows a **positive correlation**. You might also see a graph where one factor increases while the other decreases – a **negative correlation**.

Now try this

The table shows the death rate from coronary heart disease in men who smoked different numbers of cigarettes.

	Death rate			
Age group	Non-smokers	Light smokers	Moderate smokers	Heavy smokers
35–54	0.44	0.95	1.47	1.84
55–64	5.34	6.49	6.75	6.98
65–74	10.13	10.77	10.53	14.85
75 and over	15.19	20.00	22.27	24.93

(a) Describe what these data show. **(2 marks)**

(b) Describe how smoking can lead to cardiovascular diseases, such as heart attack or strokes. **(2 marks)**

Malnutrition and obesity

Malnutrition happens when a person eats too much or too little of a nutrient. Too little of some nutrients can lead to **deficiency diseases**. If there is too much energy in the diet and not enough exercise then there will be an increase in body fat. Too much body fat leads to **obesity**.

Measuring obesity

Obesity can be measured by **BMI** or by **waist : hip** ratio.

Waist : hip ratio is calculated using this equation:

$$\text{Waist : hip ratio} = \frac{\text{waist measurement}}{\text{hip measurement}}$$

People with a high waist : hip ratio ('apples') are more at risk of some diseases than those with a lower waist : hip ratio ('pears').

 Body mass index (BMI)

BMI is calculated using this equation:

$$\text{BMI} = \frac{\text{weight in kilograms}}{(\text{height in metres})^2}$$

Adults who have a BMI over 30 are said to be obese.

Obesity is linked with many health problems, including Type 2 diabetes.

CHD = coronary heart disease

As waist : hip ratio increases, the **risk** of coronary heart disease increases.

Normal waist-to-hip ratios			
	excellent	**good**	**average**
males	<0.85	0.85–0.89	0.90–0.95
females	<0.75	0.75–0.79	0.80–0.86

You don't need to know these figures. What you must be able to do is to calculate the waist : hip ratio.

Worked example

A scientific study showed that for a 10 g increase in wholegrain fibre that a person ate each day, there was a 10% decrease in their risk of developing bowel cancer. The scientists concluded that people should eat lots of wholegrain foods every day to help them stay healthy.

Do the results of this study support this conclusion? Give a reason for your answer.

(2 marks)

The results do support this conclusion, because the more fibre the person eats the lower their risk of getting bowel cancer.

You will not be expected to know the effect of fibre in the diet, but you will be expected to answer questions like this about the effect of food on health from data that you are given. You will be given data to work with.

Now try this

1 (a) A man has a waist measurement of 109 cm and a hip measurement of 112 cm.
   Calculate his waist : hip ratio. **(1 mark)**
   (b) Use the table above to explain whether the man is at a higher than average risk of developing coronary heart disease. **(1 mark)**
2 A 45-year-old woman is 160 cm high and weighs 80 kg. Calculate her BMI and state whether or not she is obese. **(2 marks)**

Cardiovascular disease

Cardiovascular disease may be **treated** using medication, surgery, or by making lifestyle changes.

Lifestyle changes

Doctors will advise the patient to:
- give up smoking
- take more exercise
- eat a healthier diet (lower fat, sugar and salt)
- lose weight.

👍 no side effects

👍 may reduce chances of getting other health conditions

👍 this is the cheapest option

👎 may take time to work or may not work effectively

Medication

If lifestyle changes do not improve the patient's health, the doctor may prescribe **medication**, such as betablockers, to reduce blood pressure.

👍 start working immediately, e.g. to lower blood pressure

👍 easy to do

👍 cheaper and less risky than surgery

👎 need to be taken long term and can have side effects

👎 may not work well with other medication the person is taking

Surgery

If an artery becomes narrowed, the drop in blood flow can cause damage to tissue beyond the blockage. A wire frame, called a **stent**, is inserted into the narrowed part of the artery.

Sometimes **heart by-pass** surgery is carried out, when a new blood vessel is inserted to by-pass blocked coronary arteries.

If the blood supply to the heart muscle is reduced or stopped, the heart muscle cells cannot get enough oxygen for respiration. This means the cells die and the person has a heart attack.

👍 usually a long term solution

👎 there is a risk the person will not recover after the operation

👎 surgery is expensive

👎 more difficult to do than giving medication

👎 there is a risk the person will develop an infection after surgery

Worked example

Surgery is usually only carried out if the person has serious heart disease and other treatments will not work. Explain why. **(2 marks)**

When anybody has surgery, there is always a risk that they may not recover, or that the surgery will cause further damage. Therefore it is safer to try making lifestyle changes first, or give the person medication. Surgery is also more expensive. However, for serious heart disease, lifestyle changes and medication are unlikely to solve the problem, so surgery can be given straight away.

You need to consider the risks and the expense of surgery.

Now try this

Give **three** lifestyle changes that a doctor might recommend to a person with heart disease.   **(3 marks)**

Plant defences

Plants have many adaptations to protect themselves from attack by **pests** and **pathogens**.
A pest is an organism that causes damage to a crop plant, e.g. plant-eating insects.

Physical barriers

Many plants have **bark** and **thick waxy cuticles** (outer covering of a leaf) that are difficult for a pest to get through. Some have adaptations such as **spikes** and **thorns** to stop pests eating them. **Cellulose cell walls** are difficult for pathogens to break down unless they produce a suitable enzyme.

Chemical defences

Plants also protect themselves from attack by producing **chemicals**. They make:
- poisons in their cells to **deter pests** that try to eat them
- chemicals that **kill pathogens** (such as bacteria and fungi), which infect them and cause disease.

Using plant chemicals

You use some of the defence chemicals found in plants as **medicines**.

Example	Plant source	Use
quinine	*Cinchona* tree	to treat human disease, e.g. malaria
digoxin	foxglove	to treat human disease, e.g. heart disease
aspirin	willow tree and other plants	to relieve **symptoms**, e.g. pain and fever

> You only need to remember the uses, not particular examples.

> A 'symptom' is what you feel when you have a disease.

Worked example

Give two ways that medicines made from plants can be used to treat people who are ill. **(2 marks)**

To treat diseases by killing pathogens in people, or to relieve symptoms such as pain or fever.

> In a question like this you do not have to write full sentences. You can use bullet points if you prefer.

Now try this

1 Explain how physical barriers can protect a plant from pests and pathogens. **(2 marks)**

2 Explain the advantage to plants of producing chemicals that deter pests or kill pathogens. **(2 marks)**

3 Which of the following is NOT useful in protecting a plant against damage by pests?
    ☐ **A** thorns and spikes
    ☐ **B** thick waxy cuticle
    ☐ **C** sunken stomata
    ☐ **D** poisons in their cells   **(1 mark)**

Extended response – Health and disease

There will be one or more 6-mark questions on your exam paper. For these questions, you will need to think scientifically and structure your answer logically, showing how the points you make are related to each other. You may wish to revise the topic for this question, which is about **evaluating treatments for heart disease**, on page 60.

Worked example

Stanol esters are made from substances found in plants. Some scientists wanted to find out if stanol esters lower blood cholesterol. They carried out an investigation in which they added stanol esters to margarine and gave it to some people. There was also a control group. The scientists measured the blood cholesterol concentration of each person at regular intervals over several months. The graph shows their results.

Explain how the scientists should have carried out this investigation to get reliable results. **(6 marks)**

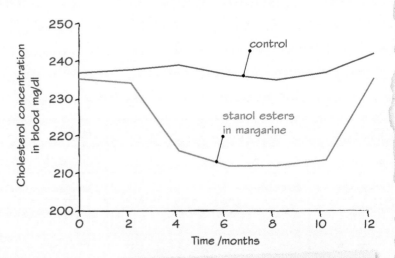

The scientists would need to carry out this investigation with a large number of people, who should be volunteers. They should be divided into two groups, matched by age and sex. One group would be given margarine containing stanol esters and the other group should be given the same margarine without stanol esters in it. The people should not know which group they are in. This is so they cannot know whether they have stanol esters in the margarine they are given. This is to avoid bias.

The scientists should measure the blood cholesterol level of each person before the investigation starts and then every month for a year. After this the scientists should assess the results from the two groups to see whether the stanol esters have reduced the blood cholesterol concentration of the people who ate that margarine compared with the people in the control group.

You might be given the results of a study like this, and be given the question 'A newspaper journalist saw these results and wrote an article entitled "Plant stanol esters in margarine reduce heart disease". Was this a correct conclusion? Give reasons for your answer.' You might be expected to note that the study only shows a reduction in blood cholesterol levels, so this does not show that there has been a reduction in heart disease. Think of other points you might make. There are other factors that should be standardized between groups, like body mass, diet and starting cholesterol level, as these also affect cholesterol levels.

Now try this

Explain how lifestyle factors might increase the chances of a person developing some kinds of cancer.

(6 marks)

Photosynthesis

Photosynthesis is the process that plants and algae use to make their own food. Plants are called **producers** because they produce their own food. Photosynthetic organisms are the main producers of food and therefore **biomass**. Biomass is the mass of living material at a particular stage in a food chain.

Photosynthesis equation

Photosynthesis can be summarised by this equation:

absorbed by chlorophyll

light energy

carbon dioxide + water ⟶ glucose + oxygen

| from air | from soil |

| a sugar | | released to air as **by-product** (not needed) |

> Chlorophyll is a green substance found in the chloroplasts of some plants.

> Remember that during photosynthesis there is an energy transfer from light energy to chemical energy stored in the sugars produced.

Worked example

A student set up six bottles. Each contained the same number of gel beads containing algae, and the same volume of hydrogencarbonate indicator solution. The indicator is yellow when carbon dioxide concentration is high, orange-red when carbon dioxide concentration is the same as in normal air, and purple when carbon dioxide concentration is low. The student placed the bottles at different distances from a lamp as shown in the diagram.

After two hours, the bottles were the colours shown in the diagram. Explain the difference in colour between bottles A and B. **(3 marks)**

Bottle A has high light intensity so photosynthesis is occurring much faster than respiration. Therefore the concentration of carbon dioxide is very low. Bottle B is too far away from the light to photosynthesise very fast, but it is respiring, so the concentration of carbon dioxide is very high.

Worked example

Explain why a leaf covered in black paper makes no food. **(2 marks)**

The black paper stops light from reaching the chlorophyll. Therefore, the leaf cannot use light energy to convert carbon dioxide and water into sugar in photosynthesis.

> Plants make food in photosynthesis, but they can only do this in the light. However, plants respire all the time, whether it is dark or light.

Now try this

1 Explain why photosynthesis is an endothermic reaction. **(2 marks)**

2 Explain the role of plants as producers of food. **(4 marks)**

> Remember that 'endothermic' reactions take in energy from the surroundings.

Limiting factors

Low temperature, dim light and low carbon dioxide concentration all limit the rate of photosynthesis. They are all **limiting factors** for photosynthesis.

Practical skills **Effect of light on rate of photosynthesis**

You can measure the effect of light intensity on the rate of photosynthesis by measuring the rate at which oxygen is given off by a piece of pondweed. You can use the apparatus shown to investigate the effect of light intensity using bright and dim lights.

Worked example

The graph shows the rate of photosynthesis of a plant at different light intensities. Explain the shape of the graph at points A and B. **(4 marks)**

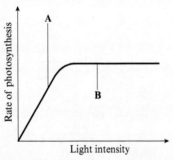

At A, light intensity is limiting photosynthesis, because increasing the light intensity increases the rate of photosynthesis. At B, light intensity is no longer the limiting factor because increasing the light intensity does not change the rate of photosynthesis. Another factor, such as carbon dioxide concentration or temperature, is limiting the rate of photosynthesis.

Increasing only carbon dioxide concentration or temperature, while keeping other factors constant, will produce a similar graph to this.

Carbon dioxide concentration

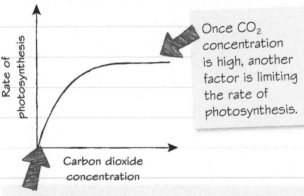

Once CO_2 concentration is high, another factor is limiting the rate of photosynthesis.

CO_2 is a limiting factor because it increases the rate of photosynthesis. There is more CO_2 to use to make sugars.

Temperature

If the temperature is too high, enzymes start to denature and the rate of photosynthesis slows down.

Temperature is a limiting factor because it increases the kinetic energy of molecules and increases the rate of enzyme activity making photosynthesis faster.

Now try this

 1 Define the term **limiting factor**.
(2 marks)

 2 Explain why measuring the oxygen given off by a plant is a way of measuring the rate of photosynthesis.
(2 marks)

Light intensity

 Practical skills You can investigate the **effect of light intensity on the rate of photosynthesis** by measuring the change in pH of solution around algal balls. The pH changes because carbon dioxide forms an acidic solution, and photosynthesis changes the concentration of carbon dioxide in the solution.

Core practical

algal balls in indicator solution

water

Aim

To investigate how light intensity affects the rate of photosynthesis.

Apparatus

- screw-top bottles (one for each distance)
- algal balls (20 per bottle)
- universal indicator solution
- measuring cylinder
- foil or black paper
- bright lamp
- small tank of water (if lamp is hot)
- metre ruler
- pH colour chart for indicator

 Change in the colour of the solution can also be measured as change in absorbance using a colorimeter.

Method

1 Place 20 algal balls and the same volume of indicator solution in each tube, and replace the screw tops.

2 Check the colour of the indicator against the colour chart and record the starting pH.

3 If using a hot lamp, place the water tank next to the lamp.

4 Use the metre ruler to place the tubes at specific distances from the lamp, on the opposite side of the tank.

5 Leave the tubes for 1–2 hours.

6 Record distance and pH of each tube, using the colour chart for identifying the pH.

 Safety: Take care if using a lamp with a hot bulb.

Using a water tank if the lamp is hot helps control for temperature, which will also vary with distance from the lamp.

Instead of distance, light intensity could be measured directly using a light meter.

Results

Draw a graph to show distance against pH.

Conclusion

As distance increases, light intensity falls and so the rate of photosynthesis decreases. This is because energy transferred by light is needed for photosynthesis to take place.

You need to be able to explain why there are the same number of algal balls in each tube, why the volume of indicator is the same, and why the bottles are all exactly the same.

Now try this

1 Explain why rate of change in pH is a measure of the rate of photosynthesis in this experiment. **(3 marks)**

2 Explain why using a water tank is important if the lamp has a hot bulb. **(2 marks)**

3 A student covered one tube of algal balls in kitchen foil and placed it close to the tank as an addition to the method above. Explain the purpose of the tube. **(2 marks)**

Specialised plant cells

Some plant cells are **specialised** to carry out specific functions.

Phloem

Phloem contains **sieve tube elements** which have very little cytoplasm so that there is a lot of space to transport sucrose and other nutrients. It also contains **companion cells** which have lots of mitochondria. These supply energy from respiration for **active transport** of sucrose into and out of the sieve tubes.

sieve plate

companion cell

sieve tube

sieve tube element

Sucrose is **translocated** around the plant in the phloem sieve tubes (see page 68 for more on translocation).

Xylem

Xylem vessels are **dead** cells which have no cytoplasm or cell contents. This means there is more space for water containing mineral ions to move through.

They have holes called **pits** in their walls to allow water and mineral ions to move out.

The walls are strengthened with **lignin** rings, which makes them very strong and prevents them from collapsing.

They have no end walls so they form a long tube that water can flow through easily.

The wall that makes the tube is made of lignin.

The diagram shows two root hairs on the outside of a root. Describe how these cells are adapted to take up water and mineral ions. **(2 marks)**

Root hair cells have long extensions that stretch out into the soil. This gives them a large surface area where osmosis can take place, which means that more water molecules can cross the cell membrane into the cell at the same time. This also gives a large surface area for mineral ions to enter the root hair cell by diffusion and active transport.

root hairs near tip of root

cytoplasm

nucleus

vacuole

soil water

cell membrane of root hair cell

cell wall of root hair cell

soil particles

Explain the meaning of the phrase **active transport**. Use minerals entering roots as your example. **(3 marks)**

Mineral salts cannot enter the root cells from soil water by diffusion because there is a higher concentration of mineral salts in the cells than in the soil. So the root cells have to use energy to transport mineral salts into the cells against their concentration gradient.

1 Explain how the structure of root hair cells is adapted to support active transport of mineral ions into roots. **(2 marks)**

2 Describe **three** adaptations of xylem vessels and explain how these adapt the cells for transporting water through the plant. **(6 marks)**

Transpiration

Transpiration is the loss of water by evaporation from the leaves. The movement of water from the roots to the leaves is called the **transpiration stream**.

Water vapour evaporates from leaves mainly through the stomata,

↑

draws water out of the leaf cells and xylem,

↑

draws water up the stem through the xylem from the roots,

↑

and causes water to enter the roots by osmosis.

Stomata

Stomata are found mainly on the lower surface of the leaf.

When guard cells take in water by osmosis, they swell and this causes the stoma to open.

When guard cells lose water, they become flaccid and the stoma closes.

The cell wall is thicker on one side of the cell than on the other.

chloroplast — vacuole

cell wall —

stoma —

— nucleus

stoma open   stoma closed

Worked example

Four similar sized leaves were cut from the same plant. The cut end of each leaf-stalk was sealed. The leaves were then covered in petroleum jelly in the following way:
A – the upper surface only was greased
B – the lower surface only was greased
C – both surfaces were greased
D – neither surface was greased.
The mass was re-measured after 24 hours and the % loss of mass of each leaf found. The results are shown in the table.

Leaf	% loss in mass
A	40
B	4
C	2
D	43

Describe and explain these results.   **(4 marks)**

Leaves A and D lost the most mass, while B and C lost very little mass. This shows that the leaves that lost the most mass were those that did not have grease on the lower surface. Leaves lose most water through the stomata which causes a loss in mass. Leaves B and C had petroleum jelly covering the stomata so they could not lose water that way. Therefore they lost almost no water.

Do not confuse transpiration with osmosis. Water enters the roots by osmosis, but transpiration is the evaporation of water that 'pulls' water up the plant.

Now try this

1 Define **transpiration**.   **(2 marks)**

2 Describe how water moves from the soil into a plant and evaporates from the leaf.   **(4 marks)**

Stomata are mainly found on the underside of the leaf because it is cooler and shadier, so less water will be lost.

Translocation

Translocation is the transport of **sucrose** and other nutrients around a plant.

Phloem

Dissolved sugars are transported around a plant in phloem.

Plants have two separate transport systems: **xylem** and **phloem**.

dissolved sucrose needed for growth in growing regions, e.g. bud

Sucrose is produced in leaves from glucose formed during photosynthesis.

Dissolved sucrose is carried around the plant in phloem.

phloem in plant veins

storage organ (e.g. potato)

dissolved sugars converted to starch and stored in storage organs so they can be used later

---

Worked example

Carbon dioxide containing radioactive carbon was supplied to a leaf of a plant as shown in the diagram.

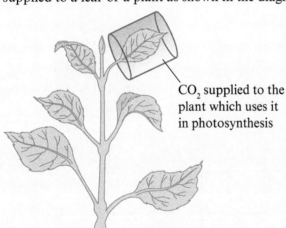

CO₂ supplied to the plant which uses it in photosynthesis

Remember that the phloem transports sugars and organic substances in the plant. See page 66 for more information.

(a) Radioactive carbon atoms will be detected in the phloem. Explain why. **(2 marks)**

The carbon dioxide will be used in photosynthesis to make glucose. Some of the glucose will be converted to sucrose which is transported round the plant in the phloem.

(b) Describe how you could use this investigation to show that sucrose can move both up and down the plant. **(2 marks)**

This will be shown if radioactivity can be detected both above and below the leaf being supplied with ¹⁴CO₂.

Now try this

1 Name the **two** transport systems found in plants. **(2 marks)**

2 An aphid is an insect pest that inserts needle-like mouthparts into the veins of a plant. It feeds on sugars.
Explain which tissue in the veins the aphid feeds from. **(2 marks)**

3 A young potato plant grows rapidly during the spring and summer. In the autumn it develops new potatoes, which are storage organs. State and explain which way sucrose moves in the phloem during the autumn, when new potatoes are developing. **(3 marks)**

Remember that sugars can be transported both upwards and downwards in a plant.

Leaf adaptations

The structure of a leaf is **adapted** for photosynthesis and gas exchange.

Leaf structure adaptations

Air surrounds most of the surface of each cell so that gas exchange can take place over most of the surface.

Epidermis cells are transparent to let light pass through to the photosynthetic cells.

Waxy cuticle is transparent to let light through.

Flattened shape of leaf gives large surface area.

The palisade mesophyll cells are packed with chloroplasts for maximum photosynthesis.

Most chloroplasts are found in the palisade mesophyll cells near the upper surface of the leaf.

cellulose cell wall

cell membrane

vacuole

vacuole membrane

chloroplast (contains chlorophyll)

nucleus

cytoplasm

Internal air spaces increase surface area for diffusion of gases.

Stomata (pores) allow carbon dioxide from air into leaf and allow oxygen from photosynthesis to leave leaf.

Xylem cells bring water for photosynthesis.

Phloem removes the sugars made in photosynthesis.

Worked example

Explain why the stomata are usually open in the day time and closed at night. **(2 marks)**

In the day time the stomata are open to allow carbon dioxide into the leaf for photosynthesis. At night the stomata are usually closed because photosynthesis does not occur unless there is light available. Closing the stomata reduces water loss.

Remember that it is one stoma but two or more stomata.

Now try this

1 Describe two features of a leaf that adapt it for photosynthesis. **(2 marks)**
2 Explain why most leaves are a thin, flat shape. **(2 marks)**
3 The leaf is adapted for photosynthesis, but these adaptations mean the leaf can lose water. Explain how. **(2 marks)**

Water uptake in plants

Environmental factors can change the rate of water uptake in plants.

Factors that affect transpiration

Factor	Effect on transpiration
light intensity	High light intensity causes the stomata to open. This increases the rate of evaporation of water from the leaf so more water is taken up to replace this.
air movement	Wind blows moist air away from the stomata, keeping the diffusion gradient high. So the more air movement there is, the higher the transpiration rate.
temperature	The higher the temperature, the more energy water molecules have, so they move faster which means a faster rate of transpiration.

Using a potometer

You can measure the **rate** of transpiration using a **potometer**.

1 Note the position of the air bubble on the ruler at the start of the investigation.

2 Note the position of the bubble on the ruler after a known number of minutes.

3 Divide the distance moved by the bubble by the time taken.

Rate of transpiration can be measured as

$$\frac{\text{distance moved}}{\text{time taken}}$$

reservoir for pushing air bubble to right-hand end of capillary tube

rubber stopper

capillary tube with scale

air bubble

Worked example

Three identical potted plants were watered and their mass recorded. Their pots were wrapped and sealed in plastic bags so that only the plant was in the open air. Each plant was then placed in different conditions. After 6 hours, the bags were removed and the mass of the plants was recorded again. The table shows the results.

 (a) Calculate the percentage change in mass for plants B and C. **(2 marks)**

Mass in g	Plant A (cool, still air)	Plant B (warm, still air)	Plant C (warm, windy)
at start	436	452	448
at end	412	398	332
% change	−5.5	−11.9	−25.9

 (b) Explain the differences in results. **(2 marks)**

The results show that evaporation of water from the plant was faster in warm air than cool air and even faster in windy air than in still air. This is because evaporation from the stomata is faster in hot and windy conditions.

Now try this

 A student places a leafy shoot in a potometer. The bubble in the capillary tube moves 50 mm in 5 minutes.

(a) Calculate the rate of transpiration in mm/min. **(1 mark)**

(b) Explain why the bubble moves faster in warmer conditions. **(2 marks)**

 (c) Describe how you would carry out this investigation to make sure the results in the two different conditions could be compared. **(2 marks)**

Think about what would make the comparison a fair one.

Plant adaptations

Plants have **adaptations** that allow them to survive in extreme conditions.

Adaptations to dry conditions

It is very hot and dry during the day in a desert. It is windy on the sand dunes, and sand holds very little water. Plants such as marram grass grow in the desert. Adaptations to their leaves help them grow there.

Marram grass lives in windy conditions on sand dunes.

You do not need to know specific examples.

rolled leaf to reduce air movement around stomata

stomata sunk in pits to reduce water loss

leaf hairs to trap moist air round stomata

waxy cuticle to reduce water loss

Adaptations to tropical conditions

Plants that grow on the ground in a tropical rain forest have to be adapted to wet conditions with low light intensity.

Adaptations include:
* large leaves to take in as much light as possible
* stems and leaves that climb up the trees to obtain more light, with the plant's roots still in the ground
* leaves with 'drip tips' so water runs off them.

Adaptations to waterlogged soil

Waterlogged soils have no air spaces so the root cells have difficulty obtaining enough oxygen for respiration. Adaptations include:
* spongy tissue in their roots that stores oxygen
* fine surface roots that take in oxygen at the water surface.

Worked example

Label the diagram to describe how the listed adaptations help a cactus to survive in a dry environment. **(3 marks)**

The cactus has no leaves which reduces water loss to air, but its green body still allows photosynthesis to take place.

Thick fleshy body stores water inside for times of drought.

Large root system collects as much water as possible from underground.

Now try this

You need to apply what you have learned to a new example.

The creosote bush lives in very hot, dry conditions in Arizona, USA. Explain how the following adaptations help it to survive.
(a) Very small leaves covered with wax. **(2 marks)**
(b) During very dry conditions its leaves fold in half and some of the leaves may drop off the plant. **(2 marks)**
(c) It has a special kind of photosynthesis that means it takes in carbon dioxide at night and stores it to use in photosynthesis by day. **(2 marks)**

Plant hormones

Plant hormones control and coordinate **plant growth** and **development**.

Tropisms

A tropism is a plant's response to a **stimulus** (a change in the environment) by growing. A **positive tropism** is when the plant grows *towards* the stimulus.
- Plant shoots show **positive phototropism** because they grow towards light.
- Plant roots show **positive gravitropism** because they grow downwards – towards the pull of gravity. (Gravitropism is also called **geotropism**.)

Auxins and tropisms

Plant hormones are chemicals that cause changes in plants. **Auxins** are plant hormones that make cells grow longer. Auxins are affected by light and cause phototropism in shoots. In a shoot, where light is coming from one side:

Auxins are produced in cells near the top of a shoot.

Auxins move to shaded part of the shoot.

shaded side of shoot

Auxins cause cell elongation.

light

lit side of shoot

Worked example

The diagram shows a germinating seed.
(a) State where the concentration of auxin is higher, A or B. **(1 mark)**

It is higher at B.

(b) Explain how this has caused the root to grow downwards. **(2 marks)**

In the roots, a higher concentration of auxin inhibits cell elongation. This means that the cells at A elongate more than the cells at B so the root grows downwards.

A high concentration of auxin stimulates cell elongation in shoot cells, but inhibits cell elongation in root cells.

shoot

A

B

root

Tropism is a **growth** response. Do not say it is movement of a plant, as that implies the plant can actually move from place to place.

Now try this

Make sure you describe the effect of light on auxin, and how this affects cell elongation, do not just link the direction of light to the curvature of the shoot.

1 Plant shoots bend towards a source of light. This is an example of a positive tropism.
   (a) Give **one** advantage of this tropism to the plant. **(1 mark)**
   (b) State which side of the shoot, lit or shaded, contains the greatest concentration of auxin. Describe the effect of the auxin on this side of the shoot. **(2 marks)**

2 Explain the advantage of gravitropism to plant roots. **(2 marks)**
3 Auxin is produced
   ☐ **A** on the light side of a plant
   ☐ **B** on the shaded side of a plant
   ☐ **C** in the root tip
   ☐ **D** in the shoot tip **(1 mark)**

Extended response – Plant structures and functions

There will be one or more 6-mark questions on your exam paper. For these questions, you will need to think scientifically and structure your answer logically, showing how the points you make are related to each other. You can revise the topic for this question, which is about **plant hormones**, on page 72.

Worked example

A student sows a seed in a pot of soil. The diagram shows what happens after the seed germinates. The shoot grows upwards and bends towards the light from a window. The roots grow downwards into the soil. Compare and contrast the responses that cause the plant to grow in this way. In your answer, name the responses and describe how they happen.

(6 marks)

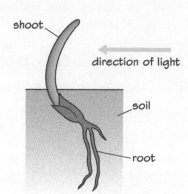

shoot

direction of light

soil

root

Command words: Compare and contrast

The question is looking for the similarities and differences between two or more things, without needing a conclusion.

The response of a plant to gravity is called gravitropism. Roots show positive gravitropism because they grow downwards. On the other hand, shoots show negative gravitropism because they grow upwards.

> The use of a connective like 'on the other hand' is a good way to introduce a difference.

The response of a plant to light is called phototropism. Shoots show positive phototropism because they grow towards the light, and roots show negative phototropism.

> The answer gives a difference between a positive and negative tropism.

Tropisms happen because of substances called auxins. These are plant hormones and they affect the way plant cells grow. High auxin concentrations stop root cells growing longer, but they stimulate shoot cells to grow longer.

> Here the answer gives a similarity and a difference between roots and shoots.

The auxin concentration is greater on the bottom side of a root, so its top side grows longer and the root bends downwards. The auxin concentration is greater on the shaded side of a shoot, so this side grows longer and the shoot bends towards the light.

> This part of the answer includes an explanation. Instead it could have just compared where, in roots and shoots, high auxin concentration and cell elongation occur.

> You need to organise your answer into a logical order, with ideas linked in a sensible way. In this answer, responses are named as required by the question, and several similarities and differences are given.

> You can revise xylem and phloem on page 66. You do not have to explain how structure is related to function when answering this question.

Now try this

Xylem and phloem are involved in transporting substances in plants. Compare and contrast these two tissues in terms of their functions and structures.

(6 marks)

Hormones

Hormones are 'chemical messengers' that target organs in the body.

Production and transport

Hormones are produced by **endocrine glands** and released into the blood. They travel around the body in the blood until they reach their **target organs**. Each hormone causes its target organ(s) to respond, e.g. by releasing another chemical substance.

Different hormones have different target organs and cause different responses.

Hormones and nerves

Nerves and hormones both help you to respond to changes in the environment and in your body. Hormones usually have a long-lived effect while nerves have a short-term effect. Nerve impulses work quickly while hormones take longer to work.

Release of hormones

Different endocrine glands produce different hormones.

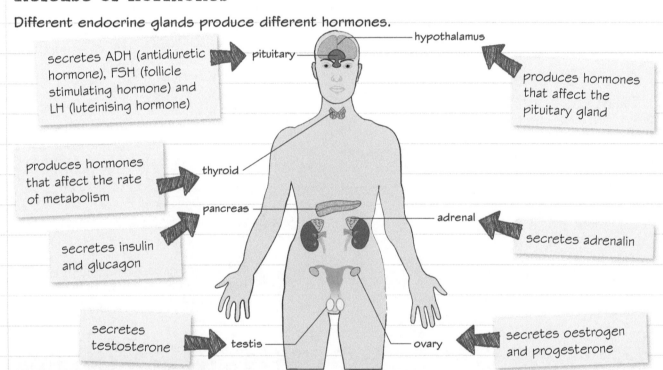

secretes ADH (antidiuretic hormone), FSH (follicle stimulating hormone) and LH (luteinising hormone) → pituitary

hypothalamus ← produces hormones that affect the pituitary gland

produces hormones that affect the rate of metabolism → thyroid

secretes insulin and glucagon → pancreas

adrenal ← secretes adrenalin

secretes testosterone → testis

ovary ← secretes oestrogen and progesterone

Worked example

Complete the table to show the target organs for each hormone.

(7 marks)

Remember: a target organ is where the hormone **acts**, not where it is produced.

Hormone	Target organ(s)
ADH	kidney
FSH and LH	ovaries
insulin and glucagon	liver, muscle and adipose tissue
adrenaline	various organs, e.g. heart, liver, skin
progesterone	uterus
oestrogen	ovaries, uterus, pituitary gland
testosterone	male reproductive organs

Now try this

 1 State what a **hormone** is.   **(2 marks)**

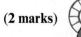 2 Give **two** differences between nervous and hormonal communication.   **(2 marks)**

The menstrual cycle

Between puberty and about the age of 50, women have a **menstrual cycle** that occurs about every 28 days. During the cycle, changes take place in the ovaries and the uterus.

If fertilisation does occur, then the uterus lining is maintained and menstruation does not happen.

Menstruation is the breakdown of the uterus lining. It begins on day 1 of the cycle and usually lasts about 5 days.

Oestrogen and **progesterone** are two of the hormones that control the menstrual cycle.

The lining of the uterus continues to build up throughout weeks 3 and 4.

During the second week, the lining of the **uterus** is gradually built up.

Days 14 to 16 are the days when **fertilisation** is most likely to take place.

Ovulation is the release of an egg from an ovary. This usually takes place around day 14.

If fertilisation occurs, the uterus lining remains thick so that the embryo can embed in the lining and obtain the nutrients it needs.

Contraception

Contraception is the prevention of fertilisation. **Hormonal contraception** includes hormone pills, implants or injections, and works by releasing hormones to prevent ovulation and thicken mucus at the cervix, preventing sperm from passing. **Barrier methods** include male and female condoms, the diaphragm, caps and sponges. These work by stopping the sperm from reaching the egg.

Worked example

Give one advantage and one disadvantage of hormonal contraceptives compared with condoms. **(2 marks)**

Hormonal contraceptives are more effective than condoms at preventing pregnancy. However, condoms protect against sexually transmitted diseases (STIs) but hormonal contraceptives do not.

Different methods have different success rates at preventing pregnancy when used correctly. Condoms = 98%, diaphragm/cap = 92–96%, hormonal methods = >99%.

Now try this

1 Explain why failure to menstruate may be the first sign of pregnancy. **(1 mark)**

2 Some women who use hormonal contraception take a pill every day. Another method is to have an implant that releases hormones slowly over a longer period of time. Suggest **one** advantage and **one** disadvantage of an implant compared with a daily pill. **(2 marks)**

Homeostasis

Homeostasis is the ability of the body to maintain a constant internal environment in response to environmental changes. **Thermoregulation** and **osmoregulation** are two features of this.

Thermoregulation

Thermoregulation is the control of body temperature. It is important because:
- If the body becomes too cold, cell reactions slow down and enzyme activity is low.
- If the body becomes too hot, enzyme activity decreases and the enzymes may be denatured.

Thermoregulation keeps core body temperature steady at around 37 °C.

Osmoregulation

Osmoregulation is the control of water content in the body. It is important because:
- If the body loses water, the solute concentration outside cells increases and the cells lose water by osmosis.
- If the body gains water, the solute concentration outside cells decreases and the cells gain water by osmosis.

You can revise **osmosis** on page 12.

How thermoregulation works

The **thermoregulatory centre** in the brain's **hypothalamus** monitors and controls core body temperature. It triggers changes in the skin and muscles.

body temperature rises due to hot environment or exercise	**hypothalamus** in brain detects rise and causes body responses	• sweat glands release more sweat onto skin surface to evaporate • sebaceous glands produce oil that helps sweat spread out over skin • energy is transferred from the skin as the sweat evaporates	increases transfer of energy to surroundings
body temperature falls due to cold environment	**hypothalamus** detects fall and causes body responses	• sweat glands stop producing sweat • body hairs raised by erector muscles in skin (causing 'goosebumps')	reduces transfer of energy to surroundings

Shivering is another response to the body temperature becoming too low. Rapid movements of the muscles transfer energy to the body by heating.

Skin structure

hair

hair muscle

epidermis

sweat gland

dermis

blood capillary

blood vessel

Describe the role of the dermis and epidermis of the skin on cooling the body. **(2 marks)**

When the body is too hot, muscles in the dermis relax, allowing hairs to lie flat. This means there is a thinner layer of insulating air trapped against the dermis.

When the body is too cold, the opposite process happens. Hairs 'stand on end', trapping a thicker layer of still air to insulate the body.

When a dog is too hot, it sticks out its tongue and pants. Suggest how this helps a dog to cool down.

(2 marks)

Blood glucose regulation

Blood glucose regulation is another example of homeostasis. The hormone **insulin** helps to control blood glucose concentration.

Pancreatic control

This is an example of **negative feedback** because a change away from the normal level (increase in blood glucose) triggers a response (release of insulin) that returns blood glucose to the normal level.

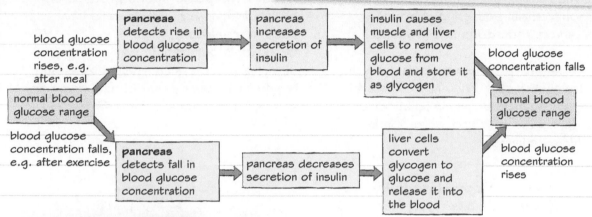

blood glucose concentration rises, e.g. after meal → pancreas detects rise in blood glucose concentration → pancreas increases secretion of insulin → insulin causes muscle and liver cells to remove glucose from blood and store it as glycogen → blood glucose concentration falls → normal blood glucose range

normal blood glucose range

blood glucose concentration falls, e.g. after exercise → pancreas detects fall in blood glucose concentration → pancreas decreases secretion of insulin → liver cells convert glycogen to glucose and release it into the blood → blood glucose concentration rises → normal blood glucose range

Worked example

The graph shows the changes in blood glucose concentration of a person who has just had a meal.

Describe what is happening. **(3 marks)**

At A the person has just had a meal, so the carbohydrates are being digested and absorbed into the blood as glucose. This causes the blood glucose concentration to increase.

At B insulin has been secreted from the pancreas which converts glucose to glycogen. Therefore, the blood glucose concentration is falling.

Remember to refer to the graph when you answer a question like this.

Worked example

A doctor wanted to test a patient's blood glucose concentration. The patient was told to have nothing to eat, and only water to drink, for eight hours before the test. Explain why.

(2 marks)

This makes sure that the glucose concentration in the blood is not affected by food or drink the person has recently consumed.

Now try this

1 Name the endocrine gland that secretes insulin, and the target organ that the hormone affects. **(2 marks)**

2 The control of blood glucose concentration is an example of negative feedback. Explain why. **(2 marks)**

It may help to look back at page 74.

Diabetes

A person who cannot control their blood glucose concentration properly has a condition known as **diabetes**. There are two main types of diabetes.

Type 1 diabetes

- **Cause**: The immune system has damaged the person's insulin-secreting pancreatic cells, so the person does not produce **insulin**.
- **Control**: They have to inject insulin into the fat just below the skin. They have to work out the right amount of insulin to inject so that the blood glucose concentration is kept within safe limits.

Type 2 diabetes

- **Cause**: The person does produce insulin but their liver and muscle cells have become **resistant** to it.
- **Control**: Most people can control their blood glucose concentration by eating foods that contain less sugar, exercising and using medication if needed.

Maths skills A person's **Body Mass Index (BMI)** is calculated using the equation:

$$BMI = \frac{weight\ (kg)}{(height\ (m))^2}$$

 You may be asked to evaluate data on the correlation between Type 2 diabetes and BMI or waist : hip ratio.

There are other factors that are linked to diabetes, apart from obesity. These include ethnic group, type of diet eaten and activity levels. The effect of exercise and diet is covered on page 59.

Worked example

 'Evaluate' here means that you have to say how strong the link is between these factors, giving reasons.

Use the graph to evaluate the correlation between obesity and Type 2 diabetes. **(3 marks)**

Sample sizes
men: 51 529
women: 114 281

 The risk of developing Type 2 diabetes increases as BMI increases. It increases faster for women than for men. The large sample sizes and the smooth curves suggest that this is a strong correlation.

Now try this

1. Explain why the dose of insulin needed by a person with Type 1 diabetes will vary, depending on the food eaten and exercise. **(3 marks)**

2. Explain why Type 2 diabetes is not usually treated by giving insulin injections. **(2 marks)**

The urinary system

The urinary system **maintains water balance**, removes excess substances absorbed from food and **removes waste products** from metabolism such as urea from the breakdown of proteins.

Structure of the urinary system

The **renal veins** carry cleaned blood back to the body.

The **renal arteries** carry blood from the body to the kidneys.

Make sure you know the difference between urea and urine, and between ureter and urethra.

The **ureters** carry **urine** from the kidneys to the bladder.

The **kidneys** remove substances including urea from the blood and make urine.

The bladder stores urine.

Urine flows through the **urethra** to the outside of the body.

A muscle keeps the exit from the bladder closed until we decide to urinate.

Urea is produced from the breakdown of excess amino acids in the **liver**. It is toxic in excess.

Inside the kidney

Each kidney contains around one million tiny tubules called **nephrons**. The nephrons make **urine**.

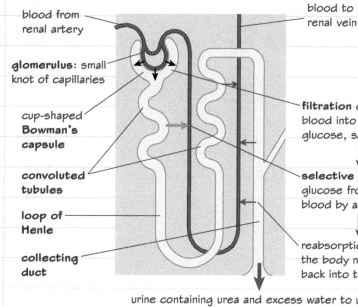

blood from renal artery

blood to renal vein

glomerulus: small knot of capillaries

cup-shaped **Bowman's capsule**

convoluted tubules

loop of Henle

collecting duct

Large molecules, such as proteins, usually cannot filter into the nephron and so stay in the blood.

filtration of small molecules from blood into tubule, including water, glucose, salts and urea

selective reabsorption of glucose from tubule back into blood by active transport

reabsorption of water that the body needs from the tubule back into the blood (**osmoregulation**)

'Selective reabsorption' is when useful molecules are absorbed back into the blood. Other molecules are left in the tubule.

urine containing urea and excess water to ureter

Now try this

1 List the structures of the urinary system that urea passes through, in order, starting with blood in the renal artery.
(2 marks)

2 Explain why a patient will die if they have kidney failure which is not treated. **(2 marks)**

Think about what is needed for 2 marks. What change will happen if a person has kidney failure? Then say why that change would be harmful.

Kidney treatments

Kidney failure is when the kidney stops working properly, so excess water, mineral ions and urea build up in the body. People with kidney failure may be treated with **dialysis**, or by **transplant** of a healthy kidney.

Dialysis

Dialysis must be carried out every 2 or 3 days, usually in a hospital.

blood flow

dialysis fluid

Dialysis tubing is partially permeable.

Diffusion restores the normal concentrations of dissolved substances in the blood.

Urea diffuses out of the blood into the fluid.

Dialysis fluid contains the same concentration of useful substances as blood so glucose and useful mineral ions are not lost.

Kidney transplant

A healthy organ such as a kidney may be donated by a **donor**, which is **transplanted** into a patient.

A healthy kidney is connected to the blood circulation, to do the work of the diseased kidneys.

Problem: The **antigens** on the transplanted kidney cells are different from antigens on cells in the patient's body.

The **antibodies** in the patient's immune system attack the transplanted kidney and **reject it**.

To prevent rejection:
- the antigens on the transplanted kidney and patient's tissues must be as similar in type as possible
- the patient must be treated for life with drugs to reduce the effects of the immune system.

This means the patient may get more infections than normal.

Antigens are proteins on the surface of cells. They are the same on all cells from one person, but differ from person to person.

Compare dialysis with the way that a healthy nephron works.   **(4 marks)**

Both dialysis and a healthy nephron remove harmful urea from the blood and control the water content of blood. Both also ensure that useful substances such as glucose and mineral ions are not lost unless they are in excess. However, a healthy nephron works all the time so the blood water concentration is controlled all the time, and urea is removed continually as well. Dialysis uses a machine, so this usually happens in a hospital. While dialysis is taking place a person is attached to the machine so cannot do very much.

Compare means giving similarities and differences.

Now try this

1   Name **two** ways that kidney failure is treated.   **(2 marks)**

2   Explain why dialysis fluid has the same concentration of glucose as the blood.   **(2 marks)**

You need to think about the composition of the dialysis fluid to answer this question.

Extended response – Control and coordination

There will be one or more 6-mark questions on your exam paper. For these questions, you will need to think scientifically and structure your answer logically, showing how the points you make are related to each other. You can revise the topic for this question, which is about the **kidneys**, on page 79.

Worked example

The kidneys are organs in the urinary system. The diagram shows the structure of one of the nephrons found in a kidney.

Explain how the structure of a nephron is related to its function in filtering the blood and forming urine.

In your answer, you should include what happens in the glomerulus and Bowman's capsule, and features that allow glucose and water to be reabsorbed back into the blood. **(6 marks)**

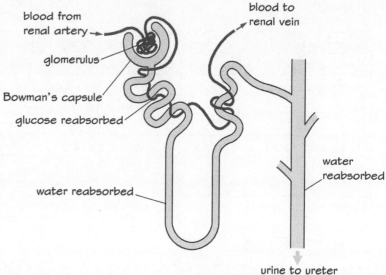

blood from renal artery →

glomerulus

Bowman's capsule

glucose reabsorbed

water reabsorbed

blood to renal vein

water reabsorbed

urine to ureter

The glomerulus is a network of tiny capillaries that carry blood from the renal artery. The cells in the glomerulus and Bowman's capsule have spaces between them. These are large enough to let small molecules such as glucose and water pass into the nephron, but small enough to stop red blood cells passing through.

The part of the nephron where glucose is reabsorbed has capillaries wrapped closely around it. This gives a large surface area where they touch. The cell membranes also have lots of tiny folds to give a really large surface area.

Water is reabsorbed in two places by osmosis. The liquid that is left is urine and it flows to the ureter. Just enough water is reabsorbed to maintain a constant water content in the blood.

The answer makes good use of information given. It could also mention that:
- the blood is under high pressure
- the glomerulus has a large surface area
- urea and salts (but not proteins) are filtered out.

The answer again makes good use of the information given. It could also mention that selective reabsorption happens and that active transport is involved.

Urine flows through the ureter to the bladder, but this is not needed to answer the question.

Your answer should show comprehensive knowledge and understanding of the topic covered. You should use the information given to you to support your answer. Organise your explanations in a structured way with clear lines of reasoning, and do not include unnecessary information.

Now try this

Thermoregulation is one way in which the human body keeps a constant internal environment. The skin can be damaged in an accident.
Suggest reasons that explain how skin damage can affect thermoregulation. **(6 marks)**

Think about nerves, receptors in the skin, and the role of hair and sweat in controlling body temperature.
You can revise the control of body temperature on page 76.

Exchanging materials

Substances such as oxygen, carbon dioxide, water, dissolved food molecules, mineral ions and urea need to be **transported** into and out of organisms.

How substances are exchanged

The table below shows different substances that need to be transported, where this happens and why.

More complex organisms

As organisms get **bigger**, their surface area to volume ratio gets **smaller**. This means they cannot rely on diffusion. They need to have specialised **exchange surfaces** and **transport systems**.

Substance	Site of exchange	Reason for exchange
oxygen	alveoli in lungs	needed for respiration
carbon dioxide	alveoli in lungs	waste product of metabolism
water	nephrons in kidney	needed for cells to function properly
dissolved food molecules	small intestine	needed for respiration
mineral ions	small intestine	needed for cells to function properly
urea	nephrons in kidney	waste product of metabolism

Worked example

(a) Complete the table to calculate some measurements relating to cubes of different side lengths. **(3 marks)**

Length of one side of cube (cm)	Surface area of cube (cm^2)	Volume of cube (cm^3)	Surface area : volume ratio
1	6	1	6
2	24	8	3
3	54	27	2
4	96	64	1.5

Adaptations for exchange

Special organs are adapted to make exchange efficient. For example, the **lungs** are adapted to exchange gases, and the **small intestine** is adapted to exchange solutes.

(b) Describe the pattern shown by these data. **(1 mark)**

As the length of one side of the cube increases, the surface area to volume ratio falls.

Maths skills Do not just talk about the surface area – it is the surface area to volume ratio that is important.

Now try this

1 Name **one** human organ that is specially adapted for exchanging substances with the environment. **(1 mark)**

2 The flatworm shown in this diagram is multicellular but it does not have an exchange system or a transport system. Explain why. **(3 marks)**

Look at the shape of the flatworm and think about its surface area to volume ratio.

Alveoli

Alveoli are adapted for **gas exchange** by diffusion between air in the lungs and blood in capillaries.

The lungs

The **lungs** are part of the breathing system. The breathing system takes air into and out of the body. In the lungs:

* oxygen diffuses from the air into the blood
* carbon dioxide diffuses from the blood into the air.

(There is more about diffusion on page 12.)

The lungs are **adapted** for efficient gas exchange.

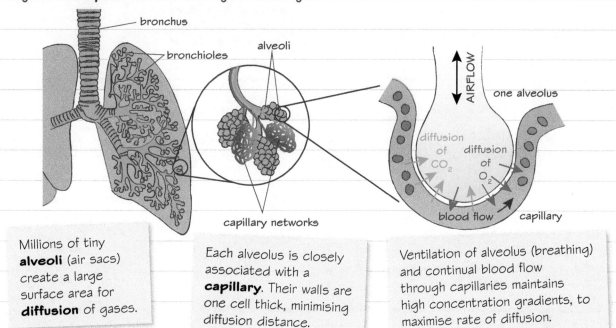

Millions of tiny **alveoli** (air sacs) create a large surface area for **diffusion** of gases.

Each alveolus is closely associated with a **capillary**. Their walls are one cell thick, minimising diffusion distance.

Ventilation of alveolus (breathing) and continual blood flow through capillaries maintains high concentration gradients, to maximise rate of diffusion.

Worked example

In some lung infections, fluid builds up inside the alveoli. Explain why this makes it harder for the person to breathe properly.   **(3 marks)**

This reduces the surface area of the alveoli over which diffusion can take place and so decreases the rate of gas exchange.

This question says 'Explain...', so your answer needs to specifically refer to how the function of the lung will be disrupted. You should try to use correct scientific language throughout.

Now try this

1. State **one** way in which the air breathed out is different from the air breathed in.   **(1 mark)**

2. People who smoke have fewer alveoli, and the alveoli are large. Explain why smokers may sometimes become short of breath.   **(2 marks)**

3. Explain the advantage of the alveoli having many capillaries around them.   **(2 marks)**

You need to consider both what the body needs to take in and what it needs to lose.

Rate of diffusion

The **rate of diffusion** across an exchange surface is affected by the structure of the surface.

Factors affecting diffusion rate

the effectiveness of an exchange surface increases with:

- increase in surface area → e.g. alveoli in lungs
- a shorter distance for diffusion → e.g. surfaces are one cell thick
- maintenance of a high concentration gradient → e.g. animals have an efficient blood supply, lungs are ventilated

The fast removal of substances maintains a steep concentration gradient so diffusion is faster.

Maths skills **Fick's law**

Fick's law is used to calculate the rate of diffusion.

For this to be as **high** as possible

...these need to be as big as possible

$$\text{rate of diffusion} \propto \frac{\text{surface area} \times \text{concentration difference}}{\text{thickness of membrane}}$$

...and this needs to be as low as possible

The symbol ∝ means 'proportional to'. Two variables are **proportional** if a change in one is always accompanied by a change in the other, and the changes are always related by a constant factor.

Worked example

People who smoke develop a disease in which the walls of the alveoli break down. These people become breathless easily. Explain why. **(3 marks)**

These people have fewer alveoli in their lungs. Therefore there is a lower surface area for diffusion, so the rate of diffusion of oxygen into their blood is lower.

You need to be able to apply the principles of Fick's law to real life situations.

Now try this

 1 Explain why an extensive capillary network and ventilation of the lungs helps to maximise the effectiveness of gas exchange.
(4 marks)

 2 An amoeba is a single-celled animal. Substances diffuse into and out of it through its cell membrane.
State what happens to the rate of diffusion if:
(a) the concentration difference is increased **(1 mark)**
(b) the thickness of the cell membrane is increased. **(1 mark)**

You do not need to give actual values, just **state** the change in the rate of diffusion.

Blood

Blood is made of four main parts: **plasma**, **red blood cells**, **white blood cells** and **platelets**. Each part of the blood has a particular **function** (job).

Blood plasma

Plasma is the liquid part of blood:
- It carries the blood cells through the blood vessels.
- It contains many dissolved substances, such as carbon dioxide and glucose.

plasma (55%)

white blood cells
and platelets (<1%)

red blood cells (45%)

White blood cells

White blood cells are larger than red blood cells, and they have a nucleus. All types of white blood cells are part of the **immune system**, which attacks pathogens in the body.

white blood cell

pathogen

Some white blood cells (**phagocytes**) surround (**ingest**) pathogens and destroy them.

Platelets

Platelets are fragments of larger cells. They have no nucleus. Their function is to cause blood to clot when a blood vessel has been damaged. The clot blocks the wound and prevents pathogens getting into the blood.

antibodies

pathogen

Some white blood cells (**lymphocytes**) produce chemical **antibodies** that attach to pathogens and destroy them.

Worked example

Explain how the structure of a red blood cell (erythrocyte) is related to its function.

(4 marks)

Red blood cells contain haemoglobin which carries oxygen. The biconcave shape of a red blood cell means it has a large surface area. This means it is easier for oxygen to diffuse into and out of the cell. The cell has no nucleus. This means the cell has room for more haemoglobin to carry more oxygen.

Biconcave means the cell is dimpled on both sides so that it is thinner in the middle than at the edges.

Now try this

1 Respiring cells need oxygen and glucose. State which parts of the blood carry each of these substances. **(2 marks)**

2 Describe **one** way in which the structure of each of the following blood components is related to its function.
   (a) phagocytes **(2 marks)**
   (b) lymphocytes **(2 marks)**

Blood vessels

There are three types of **blood vessels** – **arteries**, **veins** and **capillaries**. Their structure is related to their function.

Veins

large space for blood to flow easily back to the heart

thinner wall than artery

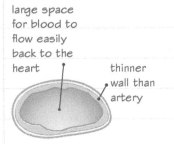

vein (cross-section)

valves to stop blood flowing backwards, so that it is returned to the heart

vein (long section)

Arteries

space where blood flows

thick wall of muscle and elastic fibres

artery (cross-section)

Exchange in capillaries

Substances are exchanged between the body cells and blood in **capillaries**. Capillaries are **adapted** for their function of exchanging substances between the blood and body cells.

capillary (only one blood cell wide)

wall only one cell thick

waste products, e.g. carbon dioxide other cell products, e.g. hormones

substances needed by cells, e.g. oxygen, glucose

Worked example

Describe the role of arteries, veins and capillaries in the human circulatory system. **(3 marks)**

Arteries carry blood away from the heart – all arteries except the pulmonary arteries carry oxygenated blood to the body. Veins carry blood towards the heart – all veins except the pulmonary veins carry deoxygenated blood from the body back towards the heart. Capillaries exchange materials, such as oxygen, glucose and carbon dioxide, with body tissues.

Remember: a key function of blood is to deliver oxygen and glucose to cells for respiration and to remove the carbon dioxide produced by respiration from cells.

Now try this

1 (a) Which is the narrowest blood vessel?

☐ **A** artery ☐ **B** capillary ☐ **C** heart ☐ **D** vein **(1 mark)**

(b) Which type of blood vessel has the thickest wall?

☐ **A** artery ☐ **B** capillary ☐ **C** vein ☐ **D** all the same **(1 mark)**

2 Explain why almost every body cell is very close to a capillary. **(4 marks)**

Think carefully about the key function of blood, and what body cells need to survive.

The heart

The **heart** pumps blood round the body. The heart and the blood vessels together make up the **circulatory system**, which delivers oxygen and nutrients such as glucose to all parts of the body.

Structure and function of the heart

Pulmonary artery carries deoxygenated blood from heart to lungs.

Aorta carries oxygenated blood from heart to body.

Vena cava brings **deoxygenated blood** from body to heart.

Pulmonary vein brings oxygenated blood from lungs to heart.

right atrium

left atrium

Valves prevent blood flowing backwards through heart (**backflow**).

left ventricle

right ventricle

Left ventricle muscle wall is thicker than right ventricle as it pushes blood all round the body.

■ deoxygenated blood
■ oxygenated blood

The sides of the heart are labelled left and right as if you were looking at the person. So the left side of the heart is on the right side of the diagram.

Remember – arteries take blood away from the heart, veins bring it back in to the heart.

Blood circulation

Valves in the heart make the blood flow in the right direction.

| Blood enters the atria. | → | The atria contract, forcing blood into the ventricles. | → | The ventricles contract, forcing blood into the arteries. | → | Blood flows through arteries to the organs and returns to the heart through veins. |

There are two circulation systems: one through the lungs and one through all the other organs.

Worked example

Explain how the structure of the heart adapts it to circulate blood effectively to the lungs and body.
(4 marks)

Blood returning to the heart from the body is low in oxygen. This enters the right side of the heart and is pumped to the lungs by the right ventricle. It becomes saturated with oxygen in the lungs. The blood then enters the left side of the heart so it does not mix with the blood that is low in oxygen on the other side of the heart.

The left ventricle has a very thick muscular wall to pump the blood all the way round the body. There is a double circulation because blood passes through the heart twice to make a complete circulation round the body, making sure the pressure of the blood never falls too low.

Now try this

1 Give **one** reason why there are valves in the heart. **(1 mark)**

2 The muscular wall of the left ventricle of the heart is much thicker than that of the right ventricle. Give **one** reason for this difference. **(3 marks)**

Aerobic respiration

Cellular respiration is a process that releases energy from glucose for use in cellular activities. The main type of cellular respiration is **aerobic respiration**, which uses oxygen.

Aerobic respiration

Aerobic respiration is a series of chemical reactions that take place mostly inside mitochondria in the cell. This is an **exothermic** process because it releases energy. This happens continuously in living cells. It is the main source of energy for cells.

Make sure you use the phrase 'releases energy' when describing the function of respiration.

broken down   releases energy

glucose + oxygen → **carbon dioxide** + **water**

a sugar   from air

The need for air makes this respiration 'aerobic'.

Use of energy from respiration

In animals:
* for metabolic processes to build larger molecules from smaller ones, e.g. proteins from amino acids, large carbohydrates (e.g. starch, glycogen) from small sugars (e.g. glucose), fats from fatty acids and glycerol
* to enable muscle contraction
* in birds and mammals, also to maintain steady body temperature in colder surroundings.

In plants and animals:
* to build larger molecules from smaller ones, e.g. sugars, nitrates and other nutrients into amino acids, which are then used to make proteins.

Worked example

The graph shows the concentration of oxygen and carbon dioxide dissolved in the water of an aquarium that contains only pond weed. Explain the shape of the carbon dioxide curve. **(2 marks)**

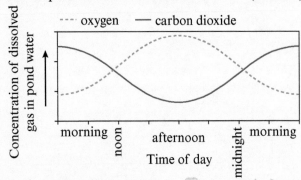

Carbon dioxide concentration increases during the evening and night because it is produced by respiration. Plants need to respire all the time. Carbon dioxide concentration falls during the hours of daylight when carbon dioxide is used in photosynthesis.

This question requires you to use knowledge about photosynthesis and respiration.

Now try this

1 Define the term aerobic respiration.
(2 marks)

2 Give **two** processes that rely on energy from respiration. **(2 marks)**

Anaerobic respiration

During exercise, energy needed for muscle contraction comes from **aerobic respiration**. If there is not enough oxygen, or aerobic respiration is not possible, **anaerobic respiration** takes place.

How anaerobic respiration works

anaerobic respiration = incomplete breakdown of glucose to release energy

→ does not use oxygen → can supply energy to muscles when there is not enough oxygen for aerobic respiration

→ in muscle cells, produces lactic acid → blood flowing through muscles then removes the lactic acid

much less energy released per molecule of glucose than during aerobic respiration

extra oxygen is required to oxidise lactic acid to carbon dioxide and water after exercise

In **plants and fungal cells**, there is a different form of anaerobic respiration that produces ethanol. However, like anaerobic respiration in animals:
- it involves breakdown of glucose
- no oxygen is used
- less energy is released per glucose molecule.

Differences between aerobic and anaerobic respiration

Aerobic respiration	Anaerobic respiration
requires oxygen	does not require oxygen
releases a lot of energy	releases much less energy
glucose broken down completely	glucose only partly broken down to lactic acid
occurs mostly in mitochondria	does not occur in mitochondria

Worked example

The graph shows how the concentration of lactic acid in the blood varies with level of exercise.

Lactic acid concentration in the blood

A

80 130 180 230 280 330 380 430
Exercise output in watts

Explain what the graph shows. **(2 marks)**

As the exercise level increases up to point A, blood lactic acid concentration stays the same. This is because the energy for the exercise is coming from aerobic respiration.

As the exercise level increases beyond point A, blood lactic acid concentration increases. This is because aerobic respiration cannot supply enough energy and the rate of anaerobic respiration increases, producing more lactic acid.

Now try this

1 Explain why human muscle cells cannot function on anaerobic respiration alone.
(2 marks)

2 Explain why anaerobic respiration releases much less energy than aerobic respiration. **(1 mark)**

Rate of respiration

Practical skills You need to understand how **the rate of respiration in living organisms can be investigated**. This experiment can use small invertebrates (e.g. maggots, woodlice) or germinating peas. See page 88 for more information on respiration.

Worked example

The diagram below shows a **respirometer**, which is used for investigating rates of respiration.

- screw clip – closed after 10 minutes
- clamp
- coloured liquid – this liquid moves as oxygen is taken up by the germinating seeds during respiration
- soda lime – absorbs carbon dioxide
- germinating seeds
- stand

(a) Explain the function of the soda lime in the respirometer. **(2 marks)**

Soda lime absorbs carbon dioxide produced by the seeds during respiration, so that it does not affect the movement of the liquid blob.

(b) Explain why the liquid blob moves during the experiment. **(2 marks)**

Oxygen is absorbed from the surrounding air by the germinating seeds. This reduces the volume of air in the container, so the blob will move towards the container.

(c) Explain how this respirometer could be used to measure rate of respiration of the seeds. **(2 marks)**

The distance that the liquid blob moves over a particular time could be measured, and a rate calculated by dividing distance by time.

Safety and living organisms

You must consider the safe and ethical use of working with living organisms. You should minimise harm to small invertebrates, and return them to their natural environment as soon as possible. You should also wash your hands thoroughly after working with living organisms.

Factors affecting respiration

Remember that respiration is affected by environmental factors, particularly temperature, and that microorganisms also respire. So the investigation will need controls.

Control for temperature – e.g. by keeping respirometers in a water bath during the experiment.

Control for something other than the study organisms affecting the gas volume – e.g. by using the same volume of an inert substance as the organisms, such as glass beads instead of seeds.

Maths skills 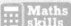 $rate = \dfrac{change}{time}$

In this case the change measured could be the amount of oxygen absorbed. In other investigations, you might measure the amount of carbon dioxide produced.

Now try this

The table shows the results of an investigation in which respirometers containing woodlice were kept at different temperatures. The uptake of oxygen in each respirometer was measured at the end of 20 min.

(a) Calculate the rate of oxygen uptake per min for each respirometer. **(2 marks)**
(b) Draw a graph to show rate of oxygen uptake against temperature. **(4 marks)**
(c) Describe the relationship shown by this experiment. **(2 marks)**

Temperature (°C)	Volume of gas absorbed in 20 min (cm³)
5	0.6
10	1.0
15	1.7
20	2.4

Changes in heart rate

On this page you will revise the formula **cardiac output = stroke volume × heart rate**.

Effects of exercise

When you exercise, your **heart rate** increases. The harder you exercise, the more your heart rate increases. Heart rate can be measured by taking your **pulse** at the wrist. It is usually measured as number of **beats per minute**.

During exercise, muscle cells are respiring faster. This means that they need more oxygen and glucose, and release more carbon dioxide. A faster heart rate means that blood is pumped faster around the body. The blood takes oxygen and glucose to cells faster and removes carbon dioxide faster.

Exercise and the heart

When you exercise, your stroke volume increases. This is because the heart muscle pumps more strongly. As more deoxygenated blood passes back into the heart, this stretches the walls of the ventricles. In time, this causes the ventricles to become thicker and more powerful, so that the stroke volume is increased even when the person is not exercising. Therefore a trained athlete, when at rest, has a lower heart rate than a non-athlete.

Worked example

The table shows the stroke volume and heart rate for two people at rest. **(2 marks)**

	Stroke volume (cm³)	Heart rate (beats per minute)
trained athlete	90	55
untrained person	60	70

Calculate the cardiac output for these two people.

athlete: 90 × 55 = 4950 cm³ per minute

untrained person: 60 × 70 = 4200 cm³ per minute

> **Maths skills** cardiac output = stroke volume × heart rate
>
> Stroke volume is the volume of blood pumped by the heart in one beat.

Now try this

1 Describe how heart rate varies with level of exercise. **(2 marks)**

> **Maths skills** Rates are always how often something happens in a particular time period. So heart rate is how many times the heart beats in a minute.

2 A person has a cardiac output of 4500 cm³ per minute and a resting heart rate of 75 beats per minute.
   Calculate their stroke volume. **(2 marks)**

3 Suggest why a trained athlete may have a similar cardiac output to an untrained person but a lower resting heart rate. **(2 marks)**

> Always show your working. This means the examiner can still give you credit for the right method even if your maths is wrong.

Extended response – Exchange

There will be one or more 6-mark questions on your exam paper. For these questions, you will need to think scientifically and structure your answer logically, showing how the points you make are related to each other. You can revise the topic for this question, which is about the **alveoli** and **rate of diffusion**, on pages 83 and 84.

Worked example

The diagram shows the structure of alveoli. Alveoli are adapted to efficient gas exchange by diffusion between air in the lungs and blood in the capillaries.

State three factors that affect the rate of diffusion. For each factor, predict how the alveoli will be adapted to increase the rate of diffusion, and give reasons for your answer.   **(6 marks)**

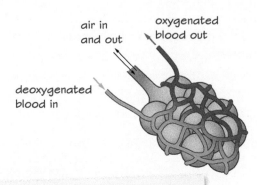

The rate of diffusion is affected by factors such as surface area, concentration difference and diffusion distance.

Fick's law shows that the rate of diffusion increases if the surface area or concentration difference increases. It also shows that the rate of diffusion increases if the thickness or the distance decreases. I expect the structure of the alveoli to be adapted to match these factors.

Without alveoli, the lungs would have a much smaller surface area. As they have millions of tiny alveoli, the surface area available for diffusion in the lungs is increased. The walls of the alveoli and the capillaries are only one cell thick. This decreases the diffusion distance to the smallest possible.

Blood leaves in the capillaries after it has gained oxygen and lost carbon dioxide. Air leaves the lungs after it has lost oxygen and gained carbon dioxide. This means that the concentration differences for oxygen and carbon dioxide are high.

A concentration difference can be described in terms of a concentration gradient.

You could use Fick's law (see page 84) to calculate differences in diffusion rates under different conditions, but this is not needed here.

The diffusion distance would be even smaller if air and blood mixed directly. However, this would cause problems including maintaining a large concentration difference.

Air enters and leaves the lungs because of breathing or ventilation. The question does not ask for any details of this process.

Now try this

You can revise blood vessels on page 86.
Answer the question using information in the diagrams, and your own knowledge and understanding.

Arteries carry blood from the heart, and veins carry blood towards the heart. The capillaries exchange substances with the body tissues. The diagram shows cross-sections through these blood vessels.
Describe how the structure of each type of blood vessel is related to its function.   **(6 marks)**

Layers: • Elastic Tissue
        • Smooth Muscle
        • Connective Tissue (Collagen)

Ecosystems and abiotic factors

Ecosystems are organised into different levels. At the level of **communities**, both **abiotic** (non-living) and **biotic** (living) factors can have an effect. You will look at abiotic factors on this page, and biotic factors on page 94.

Levels of organisation in an ecosystem

 organism

Organism is a single living individual.

 population

Population is all the organisms of the same species in an area.

 community

Community is all the populations in an area.

 ecosystem

Ecosystem is all the living organisms (the community) and the non-living components in an area.

All organisms in an ecosystem are **dependent** on other organisms for food, shelter and so on. Remember to think about the impact of this in questions about ecosystems.

Factors that affect distribution

Factors in the environment affect living organisms and their **distribution** (how widely spread they are). Changes in these factors may change their distribution.

environmental factors

living factors, e.g.
- prey
- competitor
- predator

non-living factors, e.g.
- light
- average temperature
- average rainfall
- oxygen levels in water
- pollution

A change in average temperature or rainfall may change the distribution of organisms in an area.

Oxygen levels are high in unpolluted water and low in polluted water.

A **pollutant** is energy or a chemical substance that has a harmful effect on living organisms.

Changes in non-living factors can be measured using equipment, e.g. oxygen meter, thermometer, rainfall gauge. For example, temperature affects the rates of reactions and light intensity affects the rate of photosynthesis.

Worked example

Nettle plants grow taller when they are under a large tree compared with those growing in open ground. Suggest a reason for this difference. **(2 marks)**

Under the tree, the light intensity is lower. Therefore, the plant grows taller so it has more leaves to trap available light.

There are other abiotic factors that you could suggest instead.

Now try this

The pygmy shrew is Britain's smallest mammal. It weighs only 2.3 to 5 g and its length (head and body) is only 40–55 mm. It can only live in southern Britain because the rest of the country is too cold. Explain why the pygmy shrew cannot survive in cold places. **(2 marks)**

This question is asking you to apply principles you have learned (for example, about surface area and volume ratios) to an unfamiliar example.

Biotic factors

You have seen how abiotic factors can affect communities. So can **biotic factors**. Biotic factors are factors that involve living organisms, e.g. **competition** and **predation**.

Deterring predators

Many organisms are the food of other organisms. Some animals and plants have special features that deter **predators**.

Some animals advertise that they are poisonous with very bright colours.

Some animals use colours to make them look more frightening, like these big 'eyes'.

Some plants have big thorns.

Other plants are poisonous.

Competition

Organisms need a supply of materials from their surroundings, and sometimes from other living organisms, so that they can survive and reproduce. This means there is **competition** between organisms for materials that are in limited supply.

... between plants

competition for light and space

competition for water and nutrients

... between animals

Animals may compete with each other for:
- food
- mates for reproduction
- **territory** (space for feeding, reproduction and rearing young).

Worked example

(a) In spring, a male robin will sing loudly. Explain the role of singing in robins in terms of competition. **(2 marks)**

A male robin competes with other male robins for mates (females) and for territory. Singing loudly warns other males to keep out of the robin's territory and attracts females who choose to mate with him.

> You will be expected to know the factors that organisms are competing for in a real-life situation.

(b) The ground underneath the trees in a wood is mostly bare. Explain why very few plants can grow here. **(2 marks)**

There is very little light underneath the trees in a wood. Plants are unable to compete with the trees for the sunlight.

Now try this

1 A farmer plants the seeds of his crop plants so that they are well separated from each other. Explain why. **(2 marks)**

Remember to use technical vocabulary in your answer, for example, 'competition'.

2 Milk snakes are non-poisonous snakes. Coral snakes are highly poisonous. Milk snakes that live in the same area as coral snakes have a bold red and black pattern that is similar to that of the coral snakes. Suggest the advantage to the milk snake of this patterning. **(2 marks)**

Although you may be given an unfamiliar context like this you should be able to apply principles you already know to answer the question.

Parasitism and mutualism

Parasitism and **mutualism** are examples of **interdependence** where the survival of one species is closely linked with another species.

Parasitism

A **parasite** feeds on another organism (the **host**) while they are living together. This harms the host but benefits the parasite.

Parasite	Host	Description
flea (animal)	other animals, including humans	fleas feed by sucking the animal's blood after piercing its skin
head louse (animal)	humans	head lice feed by sucking blood after piercing the skin on the head
tapeworm (animal)	other animals, including humans	tapeworms live in the animal's intestine and absorb nutrients from the digested food in the intestine
mistletoe (plant)	trees, e.g. apple	mistletoe grows roots into the tree to absorb water and nutrients from the host

Mutualism

When two organisms live closely together in a way that benefits them both, they are called **mutualists**.

> Remember to explain how **each** organism benefits in a mutualistic relationship.

Oxpecker bird benefits by getting food.

Herbivore benefits from loss of skin parasites.

The larger fish benefits from loss of dead skin and parasites.

Cleaner fish benefit by getting food.

Nitrogen-fixing bacteria in root nodules are protected from the environment and get food from the plant.

Legume plant gets nitrogen compounds for healthy growth from the bacteria.

Worked example

A tapeworm is a parasite that lives in the intestines of mammals. Explain why it is classed as a parasite. **(3 marks)**

The tapeworm depends on the host for its food supply. It absorbs digested food from the host's intestines, so it benefits from the relationship. The host is harmed because it is losing some of the nutrients in the food it eats.

> Remember mutualism is a 'win–win' relationship as both organisms benefit. Parasitism is a 'win–lose' relationship because one organism benefits but the other one is harmed.

Now try this

1 Define the term **parasite**. **(1 mark)**
2 Explain what is meant by **mutualism**. **(1 mark)**

3 Explain how the relationship between nitrogen-fixing bacteria and legumes is mutualistic. **(2 marks)**

Fieldwork techniques

The number of organisms in an area can be found using **fieldwork** techniques.

Sampling with quadrats

When studying organisms in the field, most areas are too large to count every individual organism. So we take **samples** and use them to draw conclusions about the whole area. Samples are often taken with square frames called **quadrats**.
- Quadrats are placed randomly in the area.
- The number of study organisms is counted in each quadrat.
- The number of organisms in the whole area is estimated using the equation:

number in whole area =

$$\text{mean number of organisms in one quadrat} \times \frac{\text{total area (m}^2)}{\text{area of one quadrat (m}^2)}$$

Belt transects

The effect of abiotic and biotic factors on where organisms live (their **distribution**) can be studied using **quadrats** placed along a **belt transect**.

1 m × 1 m quadrats placed at regular intervals along the transect

transect line – e.g. tape measure placed along the ground

Examples:

pond ▬▬▬▬▶ dry land

low tide on rocky shore ▬▬▬▬▶ high tide

> Choosing the number of quadrat samples to take is usually a trade-off between taking more samples (more accurate) and taking fewer samples (quicker).

Changes in **factors** (such as temperature, light intensity, trampling) are also recorded at each quadrat position. This makes it easier to link a change in distribution with a change in physical factor.

Worked example

Ten 1 m² quadrats were placed randomly on a school field that was 100 m by 200 m. The number of daisies recorded in each quadrat was: 20, 6, 33, 0, 26, 21, 18, 7, 2, and 9. Estimate the total number of daisies on the field.   **(3 marks)**

Mean number of plants per quadrat

$$= \frac{\text{total daises sampled}}{\text{number of quadrats}} = 14.2$$

Estimated number of daisies = mean × $\dfrac{\text{area of field}}{\text{area of quadrat}}$

= 14.2 × (20000/1) = 284000 daisies

> This is an estimate because if the quadrats were placed in different positions, the number sampled might be different.

> Quadrats are only useful for sampling plants, or animals that do not move about much.

> **Maths skills** To calculate the mean number of plants for one quadrat, divide the total number of plants by the number of quadrats.

Now try this

1 State when you would sample randomly with a quadrat.   **(1 mark)**

2 Describe the situation in which you would choose to sample along a transect rather than sample randomly.   **(1 mark)**

Organisms and their environment

 Practical skills   You can use **quadrats** and **belt transects** to investigate the relationship between organisms and their environment in the field. See page 96 for more information on these techniques.

Core practical

Aim

To investigate how the change in light intensity from inside a woodland to a nearby open meadow affects where cowslips grow.

Apparatus

- quadrat
- light meter
- long measuring tape

> Random sampling will not help here because you need to sample organisms in relation to how the environmental factor changes.

Method

1. Set out a measuring tape from inside the woodland out to the open meadow.
2. Take a quadrat sample at regular intervals.
3. At each quadrat sample, count the number of cowslips, and measure the light intensity.
4. Compare the number of plants with the light intensity along the transect to see how light affects where the plants live.

> An alternative to counting plants is estimating percentage coverage of the quadrat (e.g. 10%, 50%) by the species. This is useful if it is difficult to count individual plants, or if some plants are much bigger than others.

Results

The results were recorded in a table.

quadrat number	Q1	Q2	Q3	Q4	Q5
distance from woodland centre (m)	0	10	20	30	40
light intensity (lux)	2.3	2.1	3.5	9.5	13.5
number of cowslips	0	0	1	5	15

The results are displayed in this graph.

Conclusion

Cowslips seem to grow better in open meadow because the greater the light intensity the greater the number of cowslips.

> Repeating the transect several times and comparing the results for each transect would help to average out any random variation.

Now try this

In the woodland/meadow transect above, the number of primroses was also counted. The results were: Q1 2; Q2 4; Q3 7; Q4 1; Q5 0.

(a) Display these values, and the light intensity values, on one graph to show how they change over distance along the transect.
(2 marks)

(b) Describe what your graph shows about the relationship between light intensity and number of primroses. **(2 marks)**

Energy transfer between trophic levels

Energy is stored in the biomass of an organism. This energy is transferred to the next **trophic level** by feeding.

Energy transfers

Not all the energy from one trophic level is stored as biomass in the next level. Some of it is transferred to the environment. Energy that is transferred as heating is less useful to organisms as it cannot be transferred as biomass again.

Trophic levels are the feeding levels in a food chain or food web.

energy transfers

producer | primary consumer (herbivore) | secondary consumer (carnivore)

energy transferred to plant by light during photosynthesis

energy from respiration transferred to surroundings by heat

energy stored in new plant biomass which can be transferred to herbivores in their food

energy stored in biomass of food

energy from respiration transferred to surroundings by heat

energy stored in substances in faeces and urine

energy stored as new animal biomass which can be transferred to carnivores in their food

Pyramids of biomass

A **pyramid of biomass** is a diagram that shows the amount of biomass (usually as g/m²) at each trophic level in an ecosystem. The producer level is the bottom bar, and the other bars show the trophic levels in order.

The amount of biomass at each trophic level along the food chain gets smaller. This is because some energy at each level is transferred by heating the environment.

Food chains are usually no more than 4 or 5 trophic levels long because there is not enough biomass in the top level to provide the energy needed by another trophic level.

The food chain for this pyramid is:
lettuce → caterpillar → thrush

thrush | 12 g/m²
caterpillars | 60 g/m²
lettuces | 120 g/m²

The biomass of an organism is the mass of its body tissue.

Worked example

20 700 kJ of energy from the Sun's light falls on a hectare of grass in a year. The energy stored in the biomass of the grass is 1900 kJ. Find the percentage of the energy transferred by light to the plant's biomass as a result of photosynthesis. **(2 marks)**

$$\frac{1900}{20700} \times 100 = 9.18\%$$

Now try this

1 (a) Identify **two** ways that energy is transferred from an animal to the environment. **(2 marks)**

(b) Identify **one** way that energy is transferred to a plant from the environment. **(1 mark)**

2 Explain why the amount of biomass at each trophic level along the food chain decreases. **(2 marks)**

Human effects on ecosystems

Humans have positive and negative effects on **biodiversity** in ecosystems. Biodiversity is the variety of living organisms in an area.

Fish farming

Fish farming involves growing one kind of fish in an area. The fish are fed and the waste they produce is removed from their tanks.

👎 The waste can pollute the local area, changing conditions so that some local species die out.

👎 Diseases from the farmed fish (such as lice) can spread to wild fish and kill them.

👍 Farming fish reduces fishing of wild fish.

Non-indigenous species

Non-indigenous species (organisms that are not found naturally in the area) may be introduced on purpose or accidentally to an area.

👎 They may reproduce rapidly as they have no natural predators in the new area.

👎 They may **out-compete** native species for food or other resources.

👍 They may provide food for native species.

Eutrophication

Fertilisers added to fields for crops may get into streams and rivers. This adds phosphates and nitrates to the water, which is called **eutrophication**. Eutrophication can lead to loss of biodiversity in nearby water.

| Eutrophication causes water plants and algae to grow more quickly. | → | Plants and algae cover the water surface, and block light to deeper water. | → | Deeper plants cannot get light, so they die. | → | Bacteria decompose dying plants and take oxygen from the water. | → | There is not enough oxygen left in the water for fish, so they die. |

Worked example

Unionid mussels are found in many waters in the USA. Zebra mussels are small freshwater mussels that are non-indigenous species introduced to the Hudson River in 1991. The graph shows the changes in population sizes of both kinds of mussel over a 20-year period in the Hudson River.

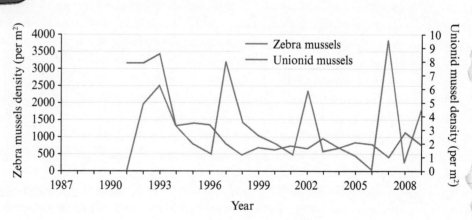

(a) Describe the changes in the unionid mussel population between 1991 and 2009. **(2 marks)**

The population falls rapidly until 1994 then more slowly until 1998. After this the population stays at approximately the same low level.

(b) The zebra mussels do not eat the unionid mussels. Suggest another reason why the zebra mussels have caused this reduction in the unionid mussel population. **(2 marks)**

They may outcompete the unionid mussels for a resource, such as food supply or breeding places.

Now try this

Focus on giving the stages that cause a decrease.

Explain how eutrophication can lead to a decrease in biodiversity. **(3 marks)**

Biodiversity

Maintaining **biodiversity** is very important, at both the **local** and **global** levels, because many organisms have important roles in ecosystems and can be useful to humans.

Reasons for maintaining biodiversity

- Moral reasons: Humans should respect other living organisms.
- Aesthetic reasons: People enjoy seeing the variety of living organisms that live in different habitats.
- Ecosystem structure: Some organisms have an important role in ecosystems, such as microorganisms in decay processes and nutrient recycling. If this planet loses species, food chains become more unstable.
- Usefulness: Some species are particularly useful to humans, for example plants that produce life-saving drugs, or wild varieties of plants grown for crops (as a source of genes if the environment changes).

Reforestation

Reforestation is replanting forests where they have been destroyed, for example to create farmland.

Advantages include:

- ✓ Restores habitat for species that are endangered. Restoring rain forest, for example, helps to conserve many species.
- ✓ Reduces the concentration of carbon dioxide in the air as the trees photosynthesise.
- ✓ Tree roots bind the soil together and reduce the effects of soil erosion.
- ✓ Affects local climate, for example reducing the range of temperature variation.

Conservation is important so that we do not lose valuable species. We can conserve organisms by protecting their habitat, preventing poaching, or keeping insurance populations in zoos and seed banks.

Worked example

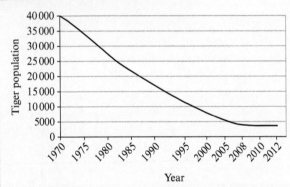

The graph shows the decline in the Asian tiger population.

(a) Calculate the percentage decrease in the population between 1970 and 2008. Show your working. **(2 marks)**

decrease = 40 000 – 3500 = 36 500

% decrease = (36 500 ÷ 40 000) × 100

= 91.25%

(b) During this time the human population in tiger regions has increased significantly. Explain how this could be linked to the decrease in tiger population. **(1 mark)**

The tigers' habitat might be being destroyed.

Another suggestion would be hunting by humans.

(c) Suggest why scientists monitor the populations of top predators such as the tiger very closely when they are assessing the biodiversity in an area. **(2 marks)**

If there are plenty of top predators, then there is plenty of energy being transferred through the food web in that ecosystem, which suggests high biodiversity.

Now try this

Farmers in the UK are encouraged to keep hedges around their fields.
Explain how keeping hedges around fields can help maintain biodiversity. **(2 marks)**

Food security

Increasing human populations need greater **food security**. This means they need to have a reliable and adequate food supply. As people become better off, there is a greater demand for meat and fish.

Effects of increased food demand

| Increasing **human population** means more food is needed. | → | The increasing demand for meat and fish means more land is used for **animal farming** and a greater impact on wild fish populations. | → | Movement of people and goods introduces new pests and pathogens to areas, damaging local crops and animals. | → | Increased waste is produced, causing more pollution. |

As well as the demand for more food, human activity has had environmental impacts that could reduce the availability of land for food production, e.g. global warming, rising sea levels, increased desertification.

Worked example

Explain the factors that farmers need to consider when using pesticides and fertilisers to increase the yield of their crops. **(2 marks)**

First of all, the farmers need to work out whether the money they get from selling the extra crops will be more than the cost of the fertilisers and pesticides. Secondly, they need to consider whether the fertilisers and pesticides will cause pollution and damage the environment in the long run.

Sustainability means being able to take what you need to live now, without damaging the supply of resources in the future.

Worked example

Growing crops to produce biofuels could be a way of reducing the use of fossil fuels and the pollution that this causes. However, some scientists think that growing biofuels is not sustainable. Explain why. **(3 marks)**

Although biofuels are renewable and do not contribute significantly to global warming, they use farmland that is needed to grow crops for food. It is possible that richer people will pay high prices for biofuels, meaning that farmers will grow biofuels instead of food crops. This could mean that poorer people cannot afford to buy food.

Now try this

Bluetongue is a viral disease of sheep and cattle. It is spread by insects. The disease causes a serious illness and many infected animals will die from it. Bluetongue is usually found in southern Europe.

(a) Bluetongue has recently spread to the UK, as shown on the map.
  (i) Suggest an explanation for why scientists think this is due to climate change. **(2 marks)**
  (ii) Give one reason why farmers in the UK are worried about bluetongue. **(1 mark)**
(b) Give one reason why pathogens like the bluetongue virus are a particular problem when they spread to a new area. **(1 mark)**

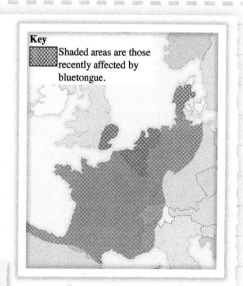

Key
▨ Shaded areas are those recently affected by bluetongue.

Think about the information you are given here about climate change, the disease being spread by insects, and how the disease has spread. You need to use this information in your answer.

The carbon cycle

Living organisms need substances from the environment. As the amount of these on Earth is limited, they are recycled through both living (**biotic**) and non-living (**abiotic**) parts of the ecosystem. The **carbon cycle** shows how the element carbon passes between the environment and living organisms.

Controls of the carbon cycle

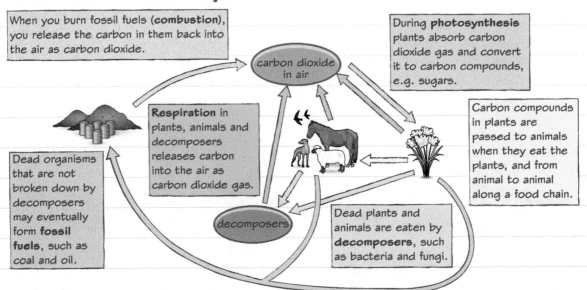

When you burn fossil fuels (**combustion**), you release the carbon in them back into the air as carbon dioxide.

During **photosynthesis** plants absorb carbon dioxide gas and convert it to carbon compounds, e.g. sugars.

carbon dioxide in air

Respiration in plants, animals and decomposers releases carbon into the air as carbon dioxide gas.

Carbon compounds in plants are passed to animals when they eat the plants, and from animal to animal along a food chain.

Dead organisms that are not broken down by decomposers may eventually form **fossil fuels**, such as coal and oil.

decomposers

Dead plants and animals are eaten by **decomposers**, such as bacteria and fungi.

In the air, carbon is part of carbon dioxide gas. In organisms, it is part of complex carbon compounds. The carbon cycle is important because it recycles carbon dioxide released in respiration to be taken in by plants in photosynthesis, to make organic molecules in living organisms.

Worked example

A large forest is cleared by burning. What effects will this have on the amount of carbon dioxide in the air (a) immediately, and (b) over a longer period? (**4 marks**)

(a) Large amounts of carbon dioxide will be released into the air by the burning (combustion) of the trees.

(b) Less carbon dioxide will be removed from the air than before because the trees would have used some for photosynthesis. So the amount of carbon dioxide in the air is likely to remain high.

Two key processes in the carbon cycle are **respiration** and **photosynthesis**. These processes are important in maintaining oxygen and carbon dioxide concentrations in the air. Combustion can change this balance.

Remember that plants photosynthesise in the light but, like all other living organisms, they respire all the time.

Now try this

1 Describe the importance of decomposers in the carbon cycle.   (1 mark)

Decomposers respire using dead plant and animal matter, releasing carbon dioxide into the atmosphere.

2 Explain the effect of respiration, photosynthesis and combustion in the carbon cycle in transferring carbon dioxide to and from the atmosphere.   (3 marks)

In each case, explain whether these release carbon dioxide into the atmosphere, or remove it.

102

The water cycle

The **water cycle** describes how water moves between different parts of our planet.

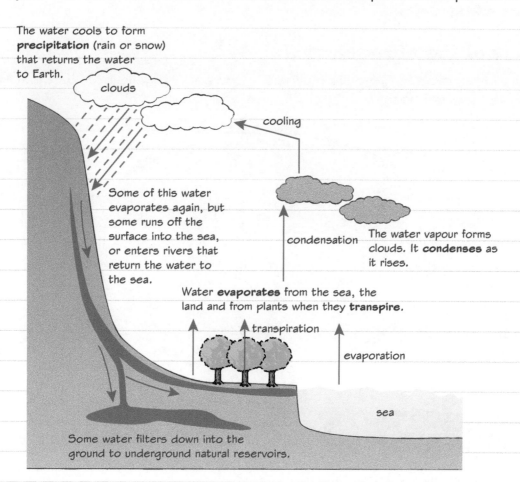

The water cools to form **precipitation** (rain or snow) that returns the water to Earth.

clouds

cooling

Some of this water evaporates again, but some runs off the surface into the sea, or enters rivers that return the water to the sea.

condensation

The water vapour forms clouds. It **condenses** as it rises.

Water **evaporates** from the sea, the land and from plants when they **transpire**.

transpiration

evaporation

sea

Some water filters down into the ground to underground natural reservoirs.

Desalination

Some areas of the world where it is hot and dry suffer **drought**. They do not get enough precipitation to use as their source of **potable** water (that is, fit to drink). If they are close to the sea, they can produce drinking water from salty water by **desalination**. One way to do this is **distillation**.

Worked example

Explain how distillation can be used to produce potable water in a village that is close to the sea. **(4 marks)**

- Salty water is heated until the water evaporates, forming steam.
- The steam is condensed in another container to give pure water.
- The salt and other impurities are left behind in the salty water.
- If renewable energy, such as sunlight, is used this saves electricity costs and avoids pollution.

Now try this

You need to describe each stage in turn.

 1 Describe the processes that take place in the water cycle. **(5 marks)**

 2 Suggest the effect on the water cycle of planting a large number of trees. **(3 marks)**

The nitrogen cycle

Plants need **nitrates** to grow well. They can get nitrates in several different ways, including through the **nitrogen cycle**.

Controls of the nitrogen cycle

A diagram of the **nitrogen cycle** shows how the element nitrogen moves between living organisms and the environment.

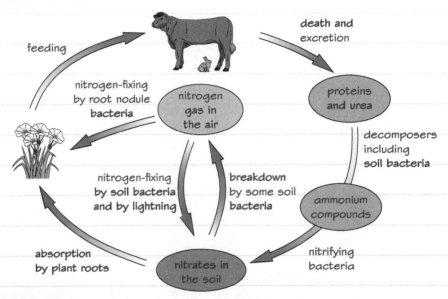

Worked example

Plants grow well in fertile soil. Explain how bacteria help to keep soil fertile. **(4 marks)**

Plants need nitrogen for making proteins but they can only take in nitrogen in the form of nitrogen compounds such as nitrates. Soil bacteria act as decomposers, releasing ammonia from proteins in dead bodies and from urea. Bacteria in the soil make nitrates. Plants can then use the nitrates to make proteins. Nitrogen-fixing bacteria in the soil and roots of some plants convert nitrogen gas from the air into nitrogen compounds that the plant can use.

In the nitrogen cycle it is important to focus on the role of bacteria.

Fertilisers and crop rotation

Farmers add **nitrates** to crop plants in **fertiliser** to help the plants grow better.

Crop rotation means growing different crops each year, on a rotation basis. This improves soil fertility (the amount of nutrients in the soil) because:

- different crops remove different nutrients from the soil
- plants such as clover have nitrogen-fixing bacteria in their roots, and can be ploughed back into the soil, to add nitrates.

The roots of clover plants contain nitrogen-fixing bacteria.

Now try this

1 Explain why a farmer might decide one year to grow clover plants in a field instead of a crop.
(2 marks)

Explain why this could be an advantage to a farmer.

2 Farmers plough crop stubble back into the soil after harvesting. Explain how this helps to improve soil fertility. **(4 marks)**

Decay

Decay is the break down (digestion) of materials by microorganisms.

Controls of decay rate

The **rate** of decomposition is affected by:

- warm temperatures because this increases enzyme activity in microorganisms
- water content because microorganisms need water for many cell processes to work
- oxygen availability because many microorganisms need oxygen for respiration.

Preventing decay

Refrigerating food makes it last longer because the temperature is too cold for most microorganisms to grow quickly.

Salting food makes it last longer because it causes water to move out of bacterial cells by osmosis, so there is not enough water in the microorganism cells for them to grow.

Packing food in nitrogen makes it last longer because it means there is no oxygen for microorganisms to respire.

Recycling kitchen and garden waste

Garden and kitchen waste can be used to make **compost**, either in the garden or by council schemes. Conditions in the compost should be controlled to encourage the growth of decay microorganisms, which grow and digest faster in conditions that are: moist, warm and aerobic (oxygen present).

Worked example

A student investigating decay set up three thermos flasks. One was filled with damp grass clippings, one with dry grass clippings, and one with damp grass clippings and disinfectant. All three thermos flasks were placed in the same room with no lids. The student weighed and recorded the proportion of clippings (in grams) that looked green on day 0 and day 6. The results are given in the table below.

Sample	Green clippings (g)		Rate of decay (g/day)
	Day 0	**Day 6**	
damp	50	5	7.5
dry	50	22	4.7
disinfectant	50	35	2.5

Complete the table by calculating the rate of decay for each sample. State which grass sample decayed most quickly and explain why. **(3 marks)**

The damp grass clippings decayed most quickly, as there was water and oxygen available, and the flask meant the temperature was warm. The dry clippings did not decay very fast as there was not enough water for microorganisms to grow. The grass with disinfectant did not decompose very much as the disinfectant killed the microorganisms.

There are different ways of measuring rate of decay (how quickly the material breaks down over time). You will be expected to calculate rate of decay from information given to you.

Maths skills

Remember:
$$\text{rate of decay} = \frac{\text{(loss of mass in grams)}}{\text{time in days}}$$

Now try this

1 Explain why compost heaps produce compost most quickly in sunny places. **(1 mark)**

2 Human bodies that are thousands of years old have been found in oxygen-deficient bogs. They show very few signs of decay. Suggest why. **(2 marks)**

Extended response – Ecosystems and material cycles

There will be one or more 6-mark questions on your exam paper. For these questions, you will need to think scientifically and structure your answer logically, showing how the points you make are related to each other. You can revise the topic for this question, which is about **human effects on ecosystems**, on page 99.

edge of field
lake

Worked example

There is a small lake in one corner of a farmer's field. The lake's surface is green.

A scientist tells the farmer that the lake is green because of eutrophication, how it happens and its effects on the lake.

Describe how eutrophication occurs, and explain the problems it causes to living things in the lake.

(6 marks)

The farmer has used fertilisers to help his crops grow well. These fertilisers contained nitrates, which washed from the field into the lake when it rained. Eutrophication is the accumulation of nitrates in the lake.

The extra nitrates in the lake cause algae to grow faster. This is why the lake's surface looks green. The algae stop sunlight reaching plants in the bottom of the lake. Without sunlight, these plants cannot photosynthesise. They die and start to decompose.

Decomposers break down the dead plants. The decomposer organisms use oxygen to respire while they do this. The amount of oxygen in the water decreases, so there is not enough oxygen for fish. The fish in the lake die because of lack of oxygen.

Command words: Describe

You need to give an account in your answer to a **describe** question. **Explain** needs a reason or justification but **describe** does not.

Nitrate fertilisers provide plants with nitrogen, needed for healthy growth. Nitrate compounds dissolve easily in water.

This part of the answer explains the problems that eutrophication can cause to plants in the lake.

This part of the answer explains the problems that eutrophication can cause to animals in the lake. Insects and other aquatic animals are also affected, leading to a loss of biodiversity.

You should think clearly about how to present your ideas before you start. Aim for a clear and logical structure. You can support this with scientific information and ideas. You should leave out information or ideas that are unnecessary to answer the question.

Remember to include at least one example of each type of relationship in your answer. You can revise parasitism and mutualism on page 95.

Now try this

The survival of some organisms depends on the presence of other species.
Using examples, compare and contrast mutualism and parasitism. **(6 marks)**

Command words: Compare and contrast

The question is looking for the similarities and differences between two or more things, without needing a conclusion.

Answers

1. Plant and animal cells

1   Muscle cells respire more (1); they need more ATP/energy (1); they carry out (aerobic) respiration/produce ATP (1).

2   any four from: cell membrane (1); nucleus (1); ribosomes (1); mitochondria (1); cytoplasm (1)

3   some cells are not exposed to light (1); named example, e.g. roots/xylem, or explanation, e.g. light does not penetrate inside plant (1)

2. Different kinds of cell

1   Similarity – any one of the following: has cell membrane/cytoplasm/DNA/ribosomes (1)

    Difference – any one of the following: no nucleus/no nuclear membrane/no mitochondria/has plasmid/has cell wall (1)

2   It has a long thin root hair/protrusion (1), which increases the surface area for absorbing water/diffusion (1).

3. Microscopes and magnification

(a)   ×400 (1)

(b)   1.2/400 = 0.003 mm or 3 micrometres (1)

4. Dealing with numbers

1   cell 0.1 millimetres (0.1 mm); chloroplast 2 micrometres (2 μm); protein molecule 10 nanometres (10 nm) (2)

2   130 micrometres (1)

3   approx. 1 μm

5. Using a light microscope

(a)   The description should cover the following points:

•   place the lowest power objective below the eyepiece

•   place the slide on the microscope stage

•   use the coarse focusing wheel to focus the image

•   if needed, move a higher power objective into place and focus using the fine focusing wheel. (4)

(b)   C (1)

6. Drawing labelled diagrams

Drawing of one red blood cell and one white blood cell using all rules described:

•   clean sharp pencil lines

•   drawn from photo

•   correct relative sizes

•   labelled to show nucleus and cytoplasm in white blood cell (no labelling expected on red blood cell)

•   labels surrounding drawing with no overlapping label lines

•   appropriate title with magnification (3 marks for all points, 2 marks for 1–3 points correct, 1 mark for 1–2 points correct.).

7. Enzymes

1   part of enzyme (1); right shape for substrate to fit in/complementary to substrate (1).

2   This means that enzymes are always at their optimum temperature (1), so that reactions occur at the fastest rate. (1)

8. pH and enzyme activity

1   (a)   rate of reaction = $\frac{1}{80}$ = 0.013 cm³/min (1)

    (b)   It took the least time for the starch/amylase mixture to react with iodine, (1), so the rate of reaction was at its fastest. (1)

2   The values of pH used are much closer together than in the first experiment, so the results should produce a more accurate value for the optimum pH. (2)

9. The importance of enzymes

1   The enzyme that digests lipids/lipase has a specific active site (1); only lipids will fit in/proteins will not fit in (1).

2   ribosomes (1)

10. Using reagents in food tests

The food contains no starch (1), some reducing sugars (1), no protein (1) or fats (1).

11. Using calorimetry

(a)   100 × 4.2 × 40 = 16, 800 J = 16.8 kJ (1)

(b)   16.8/2 = 8.4 kJ (1)

(c)   25 × 8.4 = 210 kJ (1)

12. Getting in and out of cells

1   Osmosis is the diffusion of water/net movement of water molecules from a region of higher water concentration to a region of lower water concentration (1) across a partially permeable membrane (1).

2   (a)   Neither diffusion nor osmosis need energy. (1)

    (b)   Diffusion does not need energy but active transport does need energy/diffusion takes place down a concentration gradient, active transport takes place against a concentration gradient (1).

3   water absorbed by osmosis (1); this is diffusion/passive/does not require energy (1); mineral ions absorbed by active transport (1); requires energy from respiration/cannot happen when respiration is stopped (1)

13. Osmosis in potatoes

(a)   2 marks for fully correct 1 mark for 3 or 4 right but rest wrong, OR for correct method (change in mass divided by original mass ×100%) but arithmetic error.

solution concentration (mol dm^{-3})	percentage change (%)
0.0	+22.0
0.2	+5.0
0.4	−8.0
0.6	−14.9
0.8	−24.1

(b) The solute concentration of the potato cells was just less than 0.2 mol dm^{-3} **(1)**. This is because at that concentration there would be no osmosis/net movement of water into or out of the potato cells, and so no gain or loss in mass. **(1)**

14. Extended response – Key concepts

*Answer could include the following points, to 6 marks:

Description of graph:

- As substrate concentration increases the activity of the enzyme increases.
- Reference to values at key points on the graph, e.g. activity fastest between about 75 and 85 g/dm^{-3}.
- Change in activity at different concentrations, as shown by steepness of curve.
- Change in activity is greatest where the graph line is steepest.
- Activity slows at higher substrate concentration.
- Curve flattens after about 125 mol/dm^3.

Explanation of graph:

- Starch is the substrate of amylase.
- At lower substrate concentrations, there are many free active sites on enzyme molecules.
- At lower substrate concentrations, adding more substrate means more substrate molecules can fit into free active sites and be broken down, so activity increases.
- At higher substrate concentrations, most active sites of enzyme molecules are filled with substrate molecules.
- At higher substrate concentrations, adding more substrate does not increase activity because substrate molecules must wait till an active site becomes free.

15. Mitosis

They will be identical to the parent cell **(1)**, with the same number of chromosomes **(1)**.

16. Cell growth and differentiation

1 cancer is uncontrolled cell division **(1)**; drugs stop cancer cells dividing **(1)**

2 a cell that is adapted to carry out a specific function **(1)**

3 It allows cells to become specialised **(1)** so they can carry out a function more effectively **(1)**.

17. Growth and percentile charts

1 Any one from: measure its change in height over time, measure its change in mass over time, measure the change in number and size of leaves over time (or similar) **(1)**. *The key point to mention is change over time.* If the measurements increase over time, then the plant is growing **(1)**.

2 A percentile chart compares the growth (or an aspect of growth e.g. length, body mass) of an individual **(1)** against the growth (of the same aspect) of other individuals of the same sex and age **(1)**.

3 The increase in size of a balloon is not a permanent increase in size **(1)**, while the increase in size of a child is a permanent increase in the number of cells in the child's body **(1)**.

18. Stem cells

1 an unspecialised cell **(1)** that divides to form specialised cells **(1)**

2 Cutting the top off the shoot removes the meristem **(1)**, so the growing and dividing region is removed **(1)**.

3 Embryos have to be destroyed when the stem cells are removed **(1)**; some people think it is wrong to do this because they believe embryos have a right to life **(1)**.

4 (a) Either: they are easier to extract, or they can produce more different kinds of cell. **(1)**

   (b) Adult stem cells from the patient will be recognised **(1)** but embryonic stem cells will not and the body will reject them **(1)**.

19. The brain and spinal cord

medulla oblongata; cerebral hemispheres; cerebellum; cerebral hemispheres **(2 marks for 4 correct answers, 1 mark for 3 correct answers, 0 marks for 2 or fewer correct answers)**

20. Neurones

1 Sensory neurones carry impulses from receptors to the CNS/brain/spinal cord **(1)**. Motor neurones carry impulses from the CNS/brain/spinal cord to effectors/muscles/glands **(1)**. Relay neurones carry impulses from one part of the CNS to another **(1)**.

2 The long axon and dendron of the sensory neurone means the cell can collect impulses from receptor cells and carry them through the body to the central nervous system/spinal cord/brain. **(1)**

The myelin sheath insulates the neurone from surrounding neurones and helps the electrical impulse to travel faster. **(1)**

21. Responding to stimuli

1 receptor in skin detects stimulus **(1)**; impulses pass along sensory neurone to spinal cord **(1)**; impulses pass to relay neurone **(1)**; impulses pass along motor neurone to muscle **(1)**

2 any three from: impulse reaches the end of an axon/neurone **(1)**; neurotransmitter released **(1)**; diffuses across gap and fits into receptors **(1)**; causes impulse to start/be set up in next neurone **(1)**

22. The eye

1 (a) B **(1)**

   (b) A **(1)**

2 only rods functioning in dim light/cones cannot work in dim light **(1)**; rods do not detect colour/only cones detect colour **(1)**

3 cornea refracts/bends light/helps to focus light **(1)**; lens focuses light on retina **(1)**

23. Eye problems

1 all 3 types of cone stimulated equally **(1)**

2 more than one kind of cone stimulated **(1)**; red and green cones stimulated equally **(2)** (note that second marking point on its own is awarded 2 marks)

3 lens becomes cloudy **(1)**; more diffraction of light causing less light to pass through **(1)**

24. Extended response – Cells and control

*Answer could include the following points, to 6 marks:

- receptor cells in the eye detect a stimulus
- the stimulus is the bright light/increase in light intensity
- receptor cells pass impulses to a sensory neurone
- sensory neurone passes impulses to a relay neurone
- relay neurone is in the spinal cord/central nervous system/CNS

- relay neurone passes impulse to a motor neurone
- motor neurone passes impulse to the effector/muscle in the iris
- muscle contracts/makes pupil smaller
- synapses between neurones
- chemicals carry impulse across the synapse.

25. Asexual and sexual reproduction

1 B **(1)**

2 Advantage: no need to find a mate **(1)**; disadvantage: no variation in offspring **(1)**

26. Meiosis

1 four cells produced **(1)**; haploid **(1)**; genetically different **(1)**

2 halves chromosome number so diploid number restored at fertilisation **(1)**; gametes genetically different so offspring show variation **(1)**.

3 Haploid = one set of chromosomes **(1)**; diploid = two sets of chromosomes/chromosomes are in pairs **(1)**

4 B **(1)**

27. DNA

1 (a) a piece of DNA that codes for a protein **(1)**
  (b) the entire DNA of an organism **(1)**

2 GCTA **(1)**; because A pairs with T and C pairs with G **(1)**.

3 DNA forms a double helix structure **(1)**, which consists of two strands coiled together **(1)** and held together by the weak hydrogen bonds **(1)** that link the complementary base pairs of A and T or C and G **(1)**.

28. Gregor Mendel

1 when he crossed (pure breeding) tall and dwarf peas **(1)**; offspring were all tall **(1)**

2 To make sure the results were reliable (repeatable).

29. Genetic terms

1 A chromosome is a long strand of DNA. **(1)**
A gene is a small section of a chromosome/DNA that gives the instructions for producing a particular characteristic. **(1)**
An allele is an alternative form of a gene. **(1)**

2 (a) It is heterozygous **(1)** because it has one dominant and one recessive allele **(1)**.
  (b) Purple flowers **(1)**, because purple is dominant over white **(1)**. *Remember that phenotype is what it looks like, so writing down the alleles would give you no marks for this question.*

30. Monohybrid inheritance

genetic diagram or Punnett square showing this information (any appropriate letter used):

		parent genotype Bb	
	parent gametes	B	b
parent genotype bb	b	Bb brown	bb black
	b	Bb brown	bb black

(1 mark for setting out the parent genotypes and gametes correctly, 1 mark for completing the offspring genotypes and phenotypes correctly)

The predicted outcome of phenotypes is 50% chance of brown and 50% chance of black (could also be presented as a ratio 1:1, or probability 1 in 2 for both colours). **(1)**

31. Family pedigrees

(a) heterozygous/Tt (other letters allowed) **(1)**

(b) genetic diagram or Punnett square showing offspring of Tt × tt; **(1)** 50% or 0.5 **(1)**

32. Sex determination

1 A **(1)**

2 chance is 50% **(1)**; diagram or Punnett square as shown on page 32 **(1 mark for parent phenotype, 1 for gametes, 1 for possible outcomes)**

3 There is always an X from the mother **(1)** because women are all XX and can only pass on an X chromosome **(1)**.

33. Inherited characteristics

Group A is determined by two copies of the I^A allele, or I^A alongside I^O **(1)**. Group B is determined by two copies of the I^B allele or I^B alongside I^O **(1)**. Group AB is determined by both I^A and I^B **(1)**.

34. Variation and mutation

1 Identical twins have the same genes because they come from the same fertilised egg, so characteristics controlled by genes will be the same **(1)**. Any characteristics affected by the environment may be different between the twins because different things may happen to them as they grow up **(1)**.

2 Most body cells will not contain the new allele **(1)**. Most body cells do not divide so they will not produce new cells containing the new allele **(1)**.

35. The Human Genome Project

1 any one from: doctors can find out if their patients are at risk of certain diseases **(1)**; so the patients can make lifestyle changes/doctors can find out what form of a disease a patient has **(1)**; so that patients can be given drugs to target that form of the disease **(1)**

2 They have the same genes but different alleles **(1)**, therefore a different sequence of bases in their DNA **(1)**.

36. Extended response – Genetics

*Answer should include the following points, up to 6 marks:

- parents must be heterozygous/Rr
- because some offspring have smooth coat/rr
- (smooth-coated guinea pigs) inherit one allele from each parent
- parental gametes shown as R and r
- genotypes of offspring as 1 RR : 2 Rr : 1 rr
- phenotypes correctly identified as RR and Rr rough-coated, rr smooth-coated

37. Evolution

bacteria show variation in antibiotic resistance/some bacteria are more resistant to antibiotics than others **(1)**; when antibiotics used, non-resistant die/the more resistant bacteria survive **(1)**; these reproduce **(1)**; and pass on (the gene for) antibiotic resistance to their offspring **(1)**

38. Human evolution

1 Any two suitable features, such as: increase in brain size, increase in height, upright posture and ability to walk over long distances. **(2)**

2 any two from: greater variety of tools/named examples **(1)**; made from fine flakes broken off larger stones **(1)**; more flint flaked off giving sharper edges **(1)**

39. Classification

1 The three domains are: Eubacteria, (1) Eukaryota (including plants, animals, fungi, protists), (1) Archaea (mainly bacteria living in hot/salty conditions). (1)

2 it showed that prokaryotes/bacteria need to be split into two groups (1); some bacteria/archaea have genes that work more like eukaryotes (1)

40. Selective breeding

1 Advantage: get crop plants/animals with higher yield/more meat/disease resistance etc. (1)

Disadvantage: you breed closely related organisms so they show less genetic diversity/may show genetic defects

OR

may inherit a good characteristic but also less desirable characteristics

OR

many offspring do not inherit the desired characteristics (1)

2 any three from: select parent sheep that have thick wool (1); interbreed (1); select the offspring with the thickest wool and interbreed (1); repeat many generations (1)

3 little genetic variation in the population (1); so if a new disease appears, it might spread very easily (1).

41. Genetic engineering

1 transferring a gene from one organism to another/inserting new genes into an organism/modifying the genome of an organism (1), so the desired characteristic is produced in the organism/so that the organism has a new characteristic (1)

2 advantage: greater crop yield (because weeds are killed) (1)
disadvantage: any one from: gene for herbicide resistance may be transferred to weeds (1); some people do not want to eat GM crops (1)

42. Tissue culture

1 They all come from the same parent plant. (1)
Every cell contains the same DNA. (1)

2 Take a small piece of cauliflower (1); place on agar containing nutrients and plant hormones (1); when plantlets grow put them into compost to grow bigger (1).

43. Insect-resistant plants

1 Seed for the transgenic plants costs more than seed for non-transgenic plants so farmers are less likely to be able to afford it. (1)

2 cut gene for Bt toxin out (of chromosome/bacterium) (1); using enzymes (1); insert into wheat cell DNA (1); using a vector/*Agrobacterium* (1)

44. Meeting population needs

1 Advantage: increases crop yield/less bulky to transport than manure (1)

Disadvantage: can cause eutrophication/expensive to produce (1)

2 when pest population is low, population of the biological control agent decreases (1); because there is a smaller pest population to feed on (1)

45. Extended response – Genetic modification

*Answer could include the following points, up to 6 marks:
- cut gene (for human growth hormone) from human cell
- using restriction enzyme
- cut plasmid with same restriction enzyme
- join gene to plasmid using DNA ligase
- insert plasmid into bacteria
- grow bacteria in huge fermenters
- extract bacteria and purify growth hormone.

46. Health and disease

1 bacterium (1); virus (1); fungi (1); protist (1)

2 non-communicable because it is not caused by a pathogen (1); blood clots are not spread from one person to another (1)

47. Common infections

(a) HIV or Ebola

two suitable signs for each (2), e.g.

(HIV) no signs/symptoms for a long time; flu-like symptoms on first infection; many repeated infections as immune system stops working

OR

(Ebola) diarrhoea; muscle pain; severe headache; internal and external bleeding; vomiting; fever

(b) malaria

two suitable signs (2), e.g. fever; weakness

(c) *Chalara*

two suitable signs (2), e.g. leaf loss; bark lesions/damage; dieback from top of tree

48. How pathogens spread

The mosquito is a vector because it infects the human with the parasite/pathogen. (1)

Plasmodium/the protist is the pathogen because this infects the cells and causes the disease/symptoms. (1)

49. STIs

1 sexually transmitted infections; (1)
spread by contact with sexual fluids/not using a condom during sexual intercourse (1)

2 This prevents contact with sexual fluid from his partner. (1)

50. Human defences

1 unbroken skin/mucus in breathing system (1);
lysozyme in mucus/saliva/tears OR hydrochloric acid in stomach (1)

2 skin is broken/damaged (1); so bacteria/pathogens can enter the body (1)

51. The immune system

Answer could include the following points (3):
- The pathogen has an antigen on its surface (that is unique to it).
- A lymphocyte with an antibody that fits the antigen is activated.
- This lymphocyte divides repeatedly;
  and secretes antibodies that destroy the pathogen.

52. Immunisation

1 A vaccine contains a dead or harmless form of a pathogen or antigenic material that is used to immunise a person. (1)
Immunisation means giving a vaccine to cause an immune response in the body. (1)

2 any two from: this gives the person another injection of antigens (1); increases the number of memory cells present (1); immune response greater/more antibodies made (1)

53. Treating infections

1 Antibiotics only kill bacteria/do not destroy viruses. (1)

2 bacteria die if they cannot make proteins **(1)**; but the antibiotic does not affect human cells **(1)**

54. Aseptic techniques

1 blown in from the air **(1)**; transferred by touch **(1)**; in the culture media/on the equipment **(1)**

2 so that bacteria from environment/person do not enter the culture **(1)**; so that bacteria from the culture do not contaminate person/environment **(1)**

55. Investigating microbial cultures

(a) plant extract on *x* axis, cross-sectional area on *y* with suitable units **(1)**; bar chart **(1)**

(b) In order of effectiveness in killing bacteria, from best to worst, the plant extracts are oregano, neem, thyme, lemongrass. **(1)**

56. New medicines

1 Two from:
  - B may be cheaper **(1)**;
  - A may have side-effects **(1)**;
  - patient may be allergic to A **(1)**;
  - A may not be suitable for pregnant women **(1)**;
  - A may not be compatible with other drugs the patient is taking **(1)**

2 The benefit of using animals as models is that the drugs can be tested for safety without harming humans **(1)**. A problem with using animals as models for humans is that the drugs may not work in the same way in the animal as they would do in a human **(1)**. *(Other problems may be acceptable, e.g. many people are against the use of animals for testing.)*

57. Non-communicable diseases

(a) So we can compare the different groups **(1)**, as different groups have different numbers of people in them **(1)**.

(b) (Yes) (no mark). Answer could include the following points **(2)**:

risk of cancer much higher in people with mutation;

use of figures from graph to support answer;

but only gives data for two kinds of cancer/may not be true for all cancers

58. Alcohol and smoking

1 (a) The more cigarettes smoked, the more likely a person is to die of coronary heart disease. **(1)**

The older a person is, the more likely they are to die of coronary heart disease. **(1)**

(b) (chemicals in cigarettes) make blood vessels too narrow **(1)**; increasing blood pressure **(1)**

59. Malnutrition and obesity

1 (a) 0.97 **(1)**

(b) He is at risk because the ratio is above 0.95. **(1)**

2 She has a BMI of 31 **(1)** and is obese. **(1)**

60. Cardiovascular disease

any three from: give up smoking **(1)**; exercise more **(1)**; lose weight **(1)**; eat lower fat/lower salt diet **(1)**

61. Plant defences

1 any two from: thick bark/cuticles which make it hard for pests/pathogens to penetrate **(1)**; thick cellulose cell walls that are difficult for pathogens to break down **(1)**; spikes/thorns to deter pests from eating them **(1)**

2 Pests and pathogens damage plants **(1)**; if the plant produces chemicals that protect it against attack, then the plants will be able to produce more food and so grow more rapidly **(1)**.

3 C **(1)**

62. Extended response – Health and disease

*Answer could include the following points, up to 6 marks:

Factors correctly related to a type of cancer, e.g.:
  - UV radiation/sunbathing/sunbeds can cause skin cancer.
  - Processed meat/named example linked to colon/bowel cancer.
  - Smoking linked to lung cancer.
  - Alcohol linked to mouth/pharynx/larynx/oesophageal cancer.
  - Dietary fat linked to breast cancer.
  - High salt linked to stomach cancer.

General statement that chemicals in food/cigarette smoke/pollution can cause cancer.

63. Photosynthesis

1 Energy is taken in. **(1)**

Energy in the form of light is transferred to energy in the form of chemical (potential) energy in sugars. **(1)**

2 photosynthesise **(1)**; takes in light energy **(1)**; make glucose/sugars/starch **(1)**; available for consumers to eat **(1)**

64. Limiting factors

1 Something that limits the rate of photosynthesis **(1)** when it is at a low level **(1)**.

2 Photosynthesis produces oxygen **(1)**. The more rapidly oxygen is released, the faster the photosynthesis reactions must be happening **(1)**.

65. Light intensity

1 Carbon dioxide is taken in by plants when they photosynthesise **(1)**. Removing carbon dioxide from the solution will increase its pH **(1)**. The rate of change in pH will indicate the rate at which carbon dioxide is removed from the solution **(1)**.

2 Temperature also affects the rate of photosynthesis **(1)**. If temperature is not controlled, then it will change with distance and so confuse the results. **(1)**

3 The tube will act as a control **(1)** as it should show no change in pH as there will be no photosynthesis in the tube **(1)**.

66. Specialised plant cells

1 contain many mitochondria **(1)**; supply energy from respiration/ATP **(1)**; for active transport (of mineral ions) **(1)**

2 Answer could include the following points **(6)**:
  - 1 mark for feature and 1 mark for explanation, e.g.
  - Pits in side walls; for sideways movement of water/mineral ions.
  - No cell contents; so water flow not obstructed.
  - No end walls; so water flow not obstructed.
  - Thick walls made of lignin; so cell does not collapse/is strong.

67. Transpiration

1 Movement of water through a plant **(1)** from roots to leaves **(1)**.

2 any four from: water enters root hair cell by osmosis **(1)**; moves through plant via xylem **(1)**; evaporates from leaf as water vapour **(1)**; via stomata **(1)**; draws water out of leaf cells/ xylem **(1)**

68. Translocation

1 phloem, xylem **(2)**

2 From the phloem **(1)**, because dissolved sugars are transported around the plant in phloem **(1)**.

3 downwards/from leaf to potato **(1)**; sucrose formed in leaves/in photosynthesis **(1)**; converted to starch in potatoes **(1)**

69. Leaf adaptations

1 any two from: large air spaces to supply carbon dioxide **(1)**; stomata to allow carbon dioxide into leaf/oxygen to leave **(1)**; palisade mesophyll cells packed with chloroplasts for maximum photosynthesis **(1)**; transparent cuticle to let light through **(1)**; air surrounds most of the palisade mesophyll cells to give large surface area to absorb carbon dioxide **(1)**

2 any two from: large surface area to absorb light for photosynthesis **(1)**; large lower surface of leaf for gas exchange **(1)**; thin for short diffusion pathway for gas exchange **(1)**

3 large surface area from which water can evaporate **(1)**; stomata open for gas exchange which allows water to evaporate **(1)**

70. Water uptake in plants

(a) 10 mm/min **(1)**

(b) rate of evaporation is higher **(1)**; so water travels through the shoot faster/water uptake is faster **(1)**

(c) all conditions kept the same except temperature **(1)**; one example is, e.g. air movement/light intensity **(1)**

71. Plant adaptations

(a) smaller surface area for evaporation of water **(1)**; wax to reduce water loss/make leaf waterproof **(1)**

(b) reduces surface area **(1)**, for evaporation of water **(1)**

(c) stomata open at night/closed by day **(1)**, which reduces water loss **(1)**

72. Plant hormones

1 (a) leaves become closer to the light / increased rate of photosynthesis **(1)**

(b) the shaded side **(1)**; it causes cell elongation **(1)**

2 Plant roots are positively gravitropic/grow downwards towards gravity **(1)**. Growing downwards increases the chance that the root will reach soil, which provides support, as well as water and nutrients in the soil **(1)**.

3 D **(1)**

73. Extended response – Plant structures and functions

*Answer could include the following points, up to 6 marks:

Function similarities:
- both tissues are found in roots, shoots and leaves.

Function differences:
- xylem transports water and mineral ions
- phloem transports sucrose/amino acids
- xylem carries substances in one direction only/from roots to shoots
- phloem carries substances in both directions/from source to sink.

Structure similarities:
- both tissues have a tubular shape.

Structure differences:
- xylem consists of dead cells but phloem consists of living cells

- xylem has no end walls but phloem does/phloem has sieve plates
- xylem is strengthened with rings of lignin but phloem is not
- xylem has pits in its cell walls but phloem does not.

74. Hormones

1 any two from: a chemical produced by an endocrine gland **(1)**; travels in blood **(1)**; affects target organ/cells **(1)**

2 Any two from: Hormones are chemical; nerve impulses are electrical/ionic. **(1)**

Hormones travel in blood to all parts of the body; nerve impulses travel directly to the site of action. **(1)**

Nerve impulses usually only affect one organ; hormones may affect several organs. **(1)**

Nerve impulses short-lived; hormones usually last longer. **(1)**

75. The menstrual cycle

1 If the egg is fertilised the uterus lining is maintained. **(1)**

2 advantage: implant longer lasting so don't need to remember a daily pill **(1)**

disadvantage: if the woman wants to have a baby, she has to get implant removed **(1)**

76. Homeostasis

Water/saliva from tongue **(1)**; heat lost as water evaporates **(1)**

77. Blood glucose regulation

1 gland is pancreas **(1)**, target organ is liver **(1)**

2 A change in blood glucose causes mechanisms to act that bring about the opposite change **(1)**, so that blood glucose concentration is maintained within a small range **(1)**.

78. Diabetes

1 More insulin is needed if a big meal is taken rather than a small meal **(1)**.

More insulin is needed if a meal contains a lot of sugar/ carbohydrates **(1)**.

Less insulin is needed if the person is exercising; because glucose used up in respiration **(1)**

2 person still makes insulin/has enough insulin **(1)**; but liver and muscle/body cells resistant to it **(1)**

79. The urinary system

1 kidney, ureter, bladder, urethra **(2 marks for all in correct order, 1 mark for any three in correct order)**

2 Body processes make waste products including urea **(1)**; if too much urea builds up in the blood, it becomes toxic, which will damage the body **(1)**.

80. Kidney treatments

1 dialysis **(1)**, kidney transplant **(1)**

2 so that glucose from the blood is not transferred to dialysis fluid/is not removed from blood **(1)**; by diffusion **(1)**

81. Extended response – Control and coordination

*Answer could include the following points, up to 6 marks:
- receptors damaged so they do not respond to changes in temperature
- nerves/sensory neurones damaged so they cannot transmit signals
- signals cannot reach the brain/hypothalamus
- hair lost from damaged area of skin
- no hair to stand up

- no hairs to trap an insulating layer of air (so making it more difficult to stay warm)
- sweat glands damaged/lost
- less sweat produced (so making it more difficult to cool down).

82. Exchanging materials

1 lungs **(1)**. *There are other possible answers, e.g. small intestine, kidney, but you will be expected to know about the lungs.*

2 any three from: flatworm is very flat and thin **(1)**; large surface area to volume ratio **(1)**; every cell in the flatworm is close to the surface **(1)**; can rely on diffusion **(1)**

83. Alveoli

1 any one from: less oxygen/more carbon dioxide/more water **(1)**

2 reduced surface area **(1)**; less oxygen absorbed **(1)**

3 maintains a concentration gradient **(1)**; larger surface area for exchange **(1)**

84. Rate of diffusion

1 The capillaries deliver blood that has high carbon-dioxide levels and low oxygen levels and take away blood that has high oxygen levels and low carbon-dioxide levels **(1)**. This means that there is always a concentration gradient between the blood and the air in the lungs **(1)**. Ventilation of the lungs replaces air with higher concentration of carbon dioxide and lower concentration of oxygen with air that has a higher concentration of oxygen and lower concentration of carbon dioxide **(1)**. These factors maintain a high concentration gradient between the body and air for the two gases **(1)**.

2 (a) rate increases **(1)**

(b) rate decreases **(1)**

85. Blood

1 oxygen in red blood cells **(1)**; glucose in plasma **(1)** *You must say which substance is carried by each part of the blood. In an exam, you would not get marks for just saying 'red blood cells and plasma'.*

2 (a) flexible shape **(1)**; to engulf pathogens **(1)**

(b) many ribosomes **(1)**; to produce antibodies **(1)**

86. Blood vessels

1 (a) B **(1)**

(b) A **(1)**

2 Every body cell needs oxygen and glucose for respiration, and to get rid of waste products such as carbon dioxide **(1)**. If this does not happen quickly enough then the cell may be damaged **(1)**. Capillaries are the blood vessels that exchange substances with the body cells **(1)**. A short distance for diffusion between a body cell and a capillary helps to make diffusion rapid **(1)**.

87. The heart

1 They prevent the blood flowing the wrong way in the heart. **(1)**

2 The right ventricle pumps blood to the lungs, which are not far away **(1)**. The left ventricle pumps blood out around the rest of the body, including as far as the toes and fingers **(1)**. So the left ventricle needs to pump with greater force than the right ventricle **(1)**.

88. Aerobic respiration

1 The break down of glucose to release energy **(1)** using oxygen **(1)**.

2 any two from: muscle contraction **(1)**; synthesising proteins **(1)**; maintaining body temperature **(1)**; producing fats **(1)**; producing glycogen **(1)**

89. Anaerobic respiration

1 It releases less oxygen per glucose molecule. **(1)**
It does not release enough energy for rapid activity. **(1)**

2 glucose is not fully broken down **(1)**

90. Rate of respiration

(a) Rate of oxygen uptake (cm^3/min) = volume absorbed in 20 min ÷ 20 **(1)**

5 °C: 0.03 cm^3/min

10 °C: 0.05 cm^3/min

15 °C: 0.085 cm^3/min

20 °C: 0.12 cm^3/min **(1)**

(b) suitable scales **(1)**; axes labels with quantity and unit **(1)**; axes points plotted accurately **(1)**; line or curve of best fit drawn **(1)**

(c) As temperature increases, the rate of oxygen uptake of the organisms increases **(1)**, which means that their rate of respiration increases **(1)**.

91. Changes in heart rate

1 As exercise level increases/gets more intense **(1)** the heart rate increases **(1)**. OR As exercise level reduces/gets easier **(1)** the heart rate decreases **(1)**. *It is not enough to say 'heart rate increases'. You need to link how heart rate changes as exercise level changes to get both marks.*

2 4500/75 = 60 cm^3

(2 marks for correct answer; 1 mark for correct method with arithmetic error)

3 Cardiac output is heart rate multiplied by stroke volume **(1)**. A trained athlete will have a similar cardiac output because their stroke volume is much larger **(1)**.

92. Extended response – Exchange

*Answer could include the following points, up to 6 marks:

- Arteries have thick walls to withstand high pressure.
- Arteries have muscle/elastic fibres which stretch then contract as blood passes.
- Arteries have muscle/elastic fibre to make blood flow smoothly.
- Veins have thin walls/thinner walls than arteries because blood pressure in them is lower.
- Veins have large space inside to let blood flow through easily.
- Veins have valves so blood flows one way/to stop blood flowing the wrong way.
- Capillaries are narrow/wide enough for one red blood cell.
- The walls of capillaries are one cell thick so diffusion happens quickly.

93. Ecosystems and abiotic factors

large surface area to volume ratio **(1)**; so loses a lot of heat **(1)**

94. Biotic factors

1 So that the plants do not compete **(1)** for an environmental factor such as light/water/nutrients **(1)**.

2 Predators of milk snakes may confuse them with the poisonous coral snakes **(1)** and avoid them because they know that coral snakes are poisonous **(1)**.

95. Parasitism and mutualism

1 A parasite is an organism that feeds on and causes harm to a host organism while living on or in the host. **(1)**

2 when two organisms both benefit from a close relationship **(1)**

3 The bacteria benefit from getting, e.g. glucose or amino acids from the plant and protection from the environment **(1)**. The plant benefits from getting nitrogen compounds/nitrates from the bacteria, which it needs to make proteins for healthy growth **(1)**.

96. Fieldwork techniques

1 to estimate population number/size **(1)**

2 When you want to study the effect of abiotic and biotic factors on where organisms live/to link a change in distribution with a change in a physical factor. **(1)**

97. Organisms and their environment

(a) graph with axes as for graph shown in Core practical; with primrose data correctly substituted for cowslip data **(1 mark for correct axes, 1 mark for accurately plotted points joined by straight lines) (2)**

(b) Primroses are more common where there is some light **(1)**, but not where there is a lot of light in the open meadow **(1)**.

98. Energy transfer between trophic levels

1 (a) as chemical energy in faeces and urine **(1)**
    as heat energy from respiration **(1)**

   (b) as light energy from sunlight **(1)**

2 some energy transferred to environment **(1)**; at each trophic level **(1)**

99. Human effects on ecosystems

(growth of surface plants) blocks light so plants die **(1)**; increase in bacteria uses up oxygen **(1)**; fish and other animals die **(1)**

100. Biodiversity

Any suitable answer that includes explanation of how this change would lead to increased biodiversity, such as habitat for range of species **(2)**.

101. Food security

(a) (i) bluetongue is usually found in southern Europe where it is warm **(1)** climate change is making it warmer in the UK, so bluetongue is spreading to the UK **(1)**

   (ii) any one from: more sheep and cattle will die; fewer sheep and cattle will go to market; less food for people to eat **(1)**

(b) the animals there have no immunity no resistance to it **(1)**

102. The carbon cycle

1 Decomposers release carbon back into the air as carbon dioxide from respiration. **(1)**

2 Respiration releases carbon from compounds in living organisms as carbon dioxide gas into the air. **(1)** Photosynthesis takes carbon dioxide gas from the air and converts it into carbon compounds in plants. **(1)** Combustion releases carbon from compounds in fossil fuels as carbon dioxide gas into the air. **(1)**

103. The water cycle

1 Answer could include the following points **(5)**:
- water evaporates;
- forms clouds;
- condenses into precipitation/rain;
- runs off land in rivers;
- is taken up by plants;
- filters through ground (max. 5);

2 Answer could include the following points **(3)**:
- less water available in rivers;
- less precipitation;
- less water in aquifers/drier soil
- less flooding

104. The nitrogen cycle

1 clover roots contain nitrogen-fixing bacteria, which means fewer nitrates removed from soil **(1)**; adds nutrients to the soil when clover plants ploughed in **(1)**

2 The stubble contains proteins **(1)**. Decomposers break down these proteins and release the nitrogen compounds as ammonia into the soil **(1)**. This makes the ammonia available to nitrifying bacteria, which convert it to nitrates **(1)**. Plants that grow in this soil later will be able to take in the nitrates and use them to make proteins, which they need for healthy growth **(1)**.

105. Decay

1 Warmth from the Sun will increase the rate of growth of microorganisms in the heap so they break down the materials in the heap faster. **(1)**

2 microorganisms need oxygen for respiration **(1)**; without oxygen decay microorganisms are not active/cannot break the bodies down **(1)**

106. Extended response – Ecosystems and material cycles

*Answer could include the following points, up to 6 marks:

Similarities:
- mutualism and parasitism involve two species
- they are examples of interdependence.

Differences:
- mutualism benefits both species but parasitism only benefits the parasite/does not benefit the host
- behaviour of the parasite can damage the host/cause it to die.

Examples of mutualism (at least one given):
- oxpecker and gazelle
- oxpecker gets food, gazelle gets rid of skin parasites
- cleaner fish and shark
- cleaner fish get food, shark gets rid of dead skin/parasites
- nitrogen-fixing bacteria and legume plant
- bacteria protected from the environment/get food from the plant, plant gets nitrogen compounds.

Examples of parasitism (at least one given):
- flea/headlouse feeds on the blood of other organisms
- tapeworm absorbs nutrients from food in the host's intestine
- mistletoe absorbs nutrients from host plant.

Your own notes

Your own notes

Your own notes

Published by Pearson Education Limited, 80 Strand, London, WC2R 0RL.

www.pearsonschoolsandfecolleges.co.uk

Copies of official specifications for all Pearson qualifications may be found on the website: qualifications.pearson.com

Text and Illustrations © Pearson Education Limited 2017
Produced, typeset and illustrated by Phoenix Photosetting
Cover illustration by Miriam Sturdee

The rights of Pauline Lowrie and Sue Kearsey to be identified as authors of this work have been asserted by them in accordance with the Copyright, Designs and Patents Act 1988.

First published 2017

24
10

British Library Cataloguing in Publication Data
A catalogue record for this book is available from the British Library

ISBN 978 1 292 13174 0

Printed and bound by CPI Group (UK) Ltd, Croydon, CR0 4YY

Acknowledgements

The publishers are grateful to Nigel Saunders for his help and advice with this book.

The authors and publisher would like to thank the following individuals and organisations for permission to reproduce copyright material:

Photographs:
(Key: b-bottom; c-centre; l-left; r-right; t-top)

Bridgeman Art Library Ltd: Musee de Picardie, Amiens, France 38bl, Musee des Antiquities Nationales, St. Germain-en-laye, France 38bc; **Fotolia.com:** joris17 45; **Science Photo Library Ltd:** Herve Conge, ISM 6cl, Steve Gschmeissner 6br

All other images © Pearson Education

Figures
Figure on page 58 from The incidence of liver disease and the mean ethanol consumption per person per year for different countries. Copyright © 2009 Molecular Diversity Preservation International, Basel, Switzerland. Relationship between Dietary Beef, Fat, and Pork and Alcoholic Cirrhosis by Francis Stephen Bridges; Figure on page 99 from Native Unionid and Zebra mussels, Cary Institute of Ecosystem Studies. Original material available at http://www.caryinstitute.org/discover-ecology Graph on page 62 is based on data from NHS Immunisation Statistics England 2013–14/ Figure 5: MMR coverage at 24 months; Source: COVER, Health and Social Care information Centre.